Marlette Water System

Marlette Lake
to Virginia City, Nevada
and Surrounding Area

by Julie Michler

Splash Books
Reno, NV
LrpNv.com

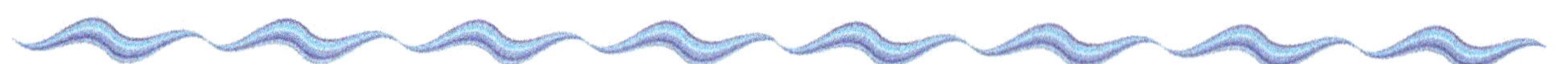

For permissions, information, or additional copies, contact juliemichler@yahoo.com

Photography and captions by Julie Michler, except as noted.
Color photos taken between 2018-2020 by Julie Michler
Black/White photographs courtesy of Marlette Water System

Author photograph by Dan Webster

Cover photograph – Washoe Lake taken from Pipe Line Road

ISBN   978-1-93881434-1

Library of Congress Control Number: 2021909798

Splash Books, an imprint of LeRue Press, LLC, Reno, Nevada

Dedication

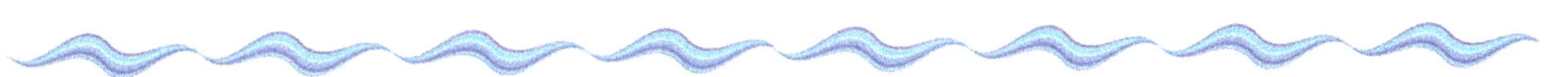

This book is dedicated to Dan Webster, my partner. Because of his experience in four wheel driving we were able to get to all of the historical sites in this area. Also, his knowledge of history was a great help in putting this book together.

Acknowledgement

I would like to thank the crew of the Marlette Water System for all of their help. Without their expertise and knowledge I would not have been able to produce this book.

These men provided access to and historical information on the water system.

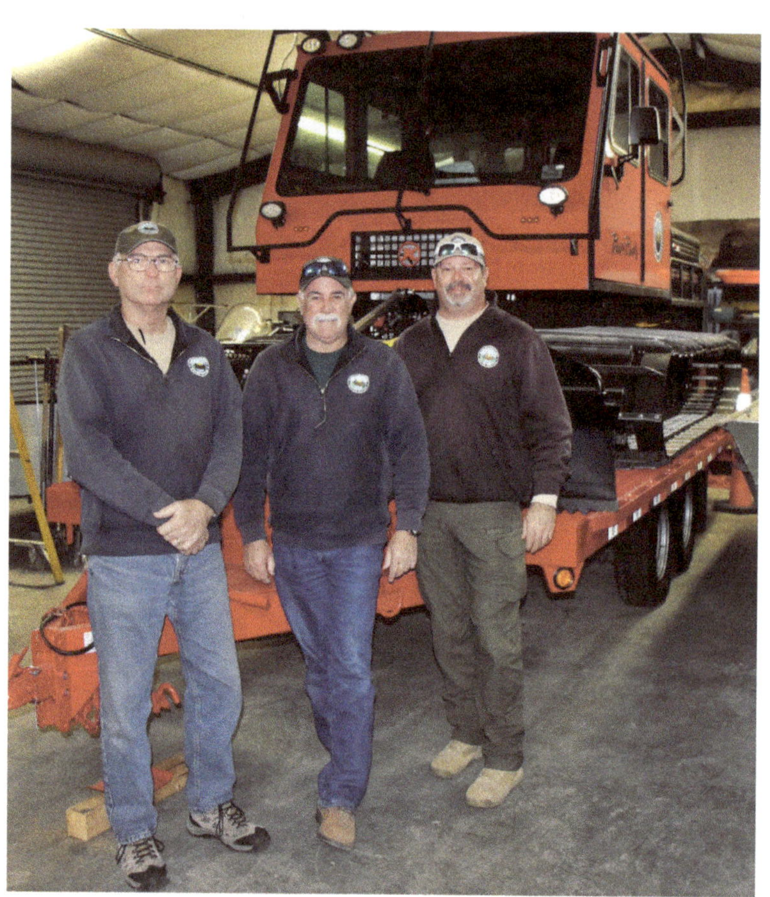

Left to right: Jeff Wohlgemuth, Water Systems Operator I; Jerry Walker, Water Systems Manager; and Blake Gudmundson, Water Systems Operator II

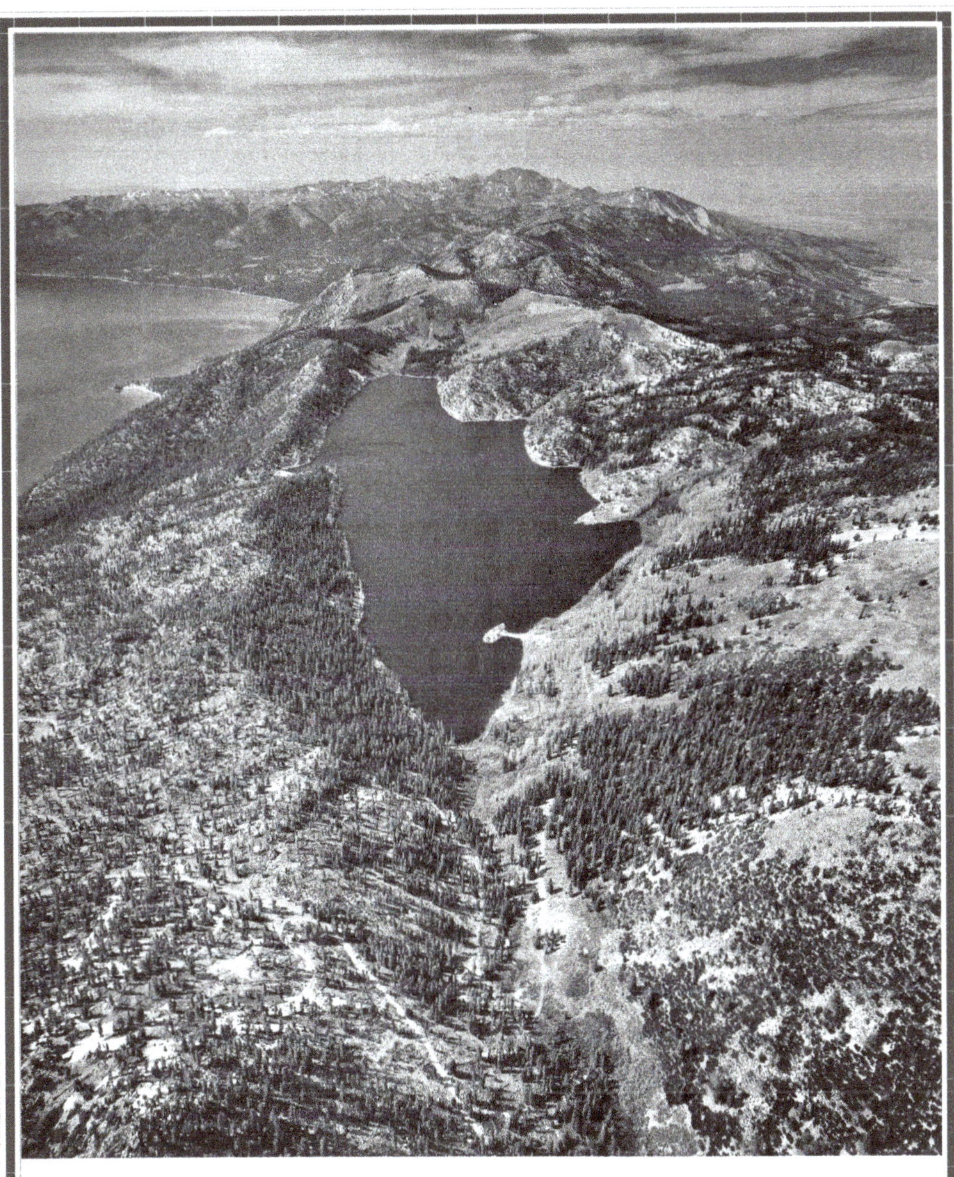

Frontispiece.   Aerial view of Marlette Lake, May 31, 1968.   Courtesy Robert S. Leighton, Sierra Pacific Power Company; provided by Millard-Spink Associates, Inc. of Nevada.

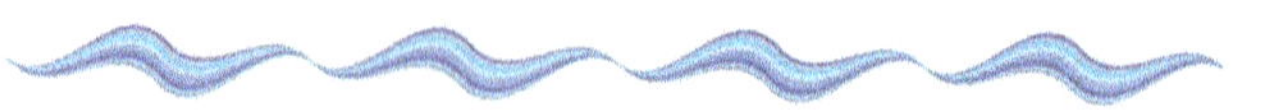

About Marlette Water Systems

Prior to May 1862, Virginia City, Gold Hill and Silver City's water was supplied by the Virginia Water Company and the Gold Hill Water Company. The water was pure and it came from the tunnels the prospectors had cut into the mountain. Water was stored in wooden tanks and sent through pipes into the towns.

Virginia City had become America's greatest producer of high grade silver and gold ore. On May 12, 1862 the water companies combined to form the Virginia and Gold Hill Water Company. In the early 1870's the Virginia and Gold Hill Water Company realized they needed more water to supply the cities domestic and mining needs as a drought was starting to threaten the cities.

In 1871 the water company consulted Hermann Schussler to develop a plan to bring water from sources in the Sierra Nevada Mountains. The purpose of the water system would be to supply water to Virginia City, Gold Hill, Silver City (the Comstock) and some for Carson City. This would be the highest pressure pipeline (inverted siphon) in the world at that time. It needed to withstand pressures of 800 pounds per square inch. Normally it would operate at 700 pounds per square inch..

In 1873 a contract was given to Hermann Schussler to design the pipeline system from Hobart Creek Reservoir to Virginia City.

- The owner of the water system changed hands a few times.
- 1870's Virginia and Gold Hill Water Company
- 1933 Virginia City Water Company
- August 8, 1957 Curtis Wright Corporation
- December 2, 1957 Marlette Water Company
- June 23, 1963 the State of Nevada purchased the system for $1.65 million

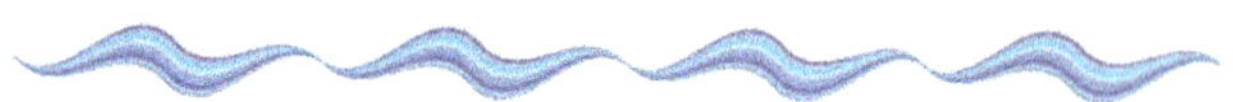

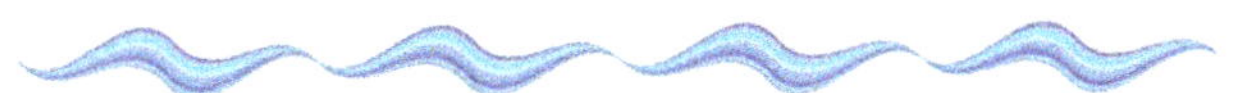

Facts

Building the water system involved 21.47 miles of pipeline. 45.73 miles of flumes and a 3,994 foot incline tunnel and over 12,020 acre feet of reservoir storage capacity (3,916,729,020 gallons of water).

The system was capable of delivering about six million gallons of water per day.

The laying of pipe and flumes (over seven miles of very rough terrain in just six weeks) was a remarkable feat considering that all labor was performed by men and mules.

The first pipeline was built in 1872 and 1873. It included a diversion dam on Hobart Creek, wooden flumes and a siphon to carry the water to tanks above Virginia City, Gold Hill and Silver City. The area still needed more water.

The second pipeline was began in 1875 and water reached Virginia City through it in 1877. This pipeline included a connection to Marlette Lake.

A third pipeline was completed in 1887. This included the North Flume from the west portal of the Incline Tunnel at Third Creek, which was more than eight miles long. The water from this flume was used to carry lumber and cord wood to Lakeview, where it was put on trains bound for Virginia City.

In 2020 the system distributed approximately 52,108 gallons to Carson City and 76,745 gallons to the Virginia City, Gold Hill and Silver Hill area.

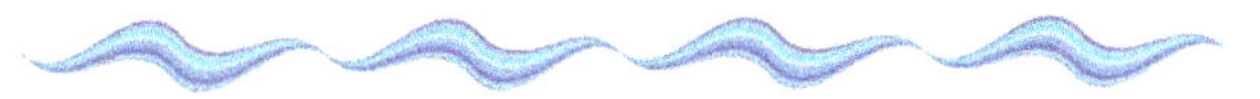

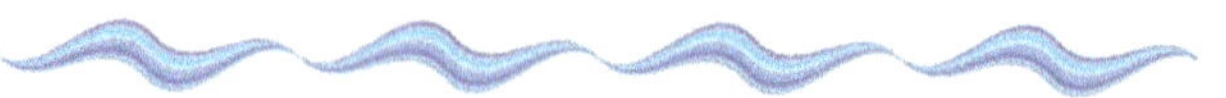

Hobart Creek Reservoir
(Hobart Creek)

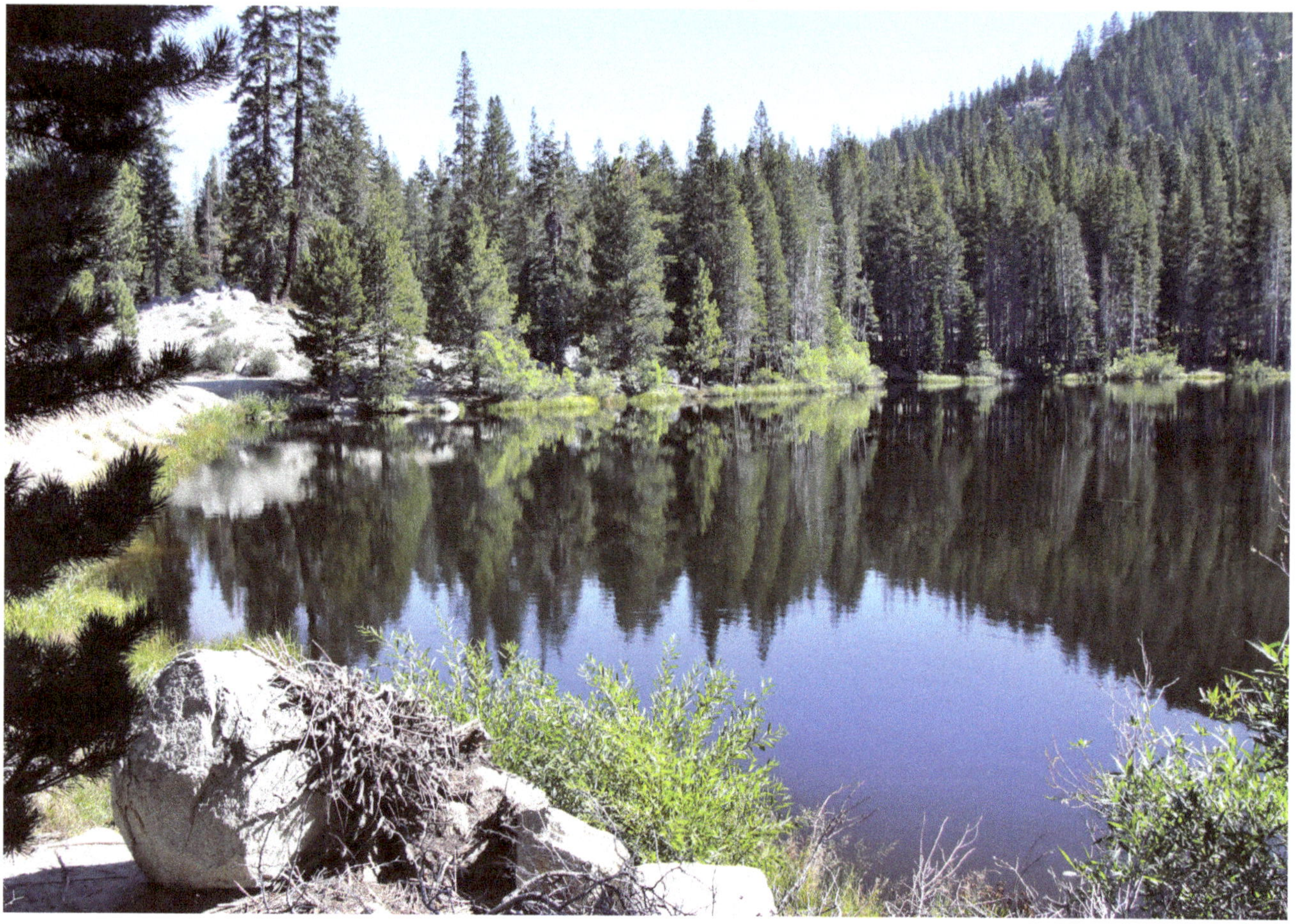

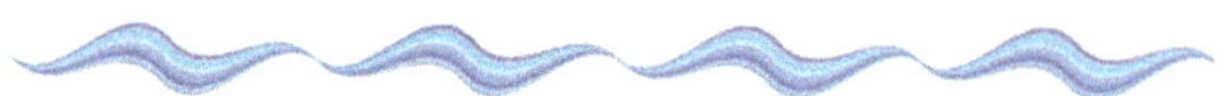

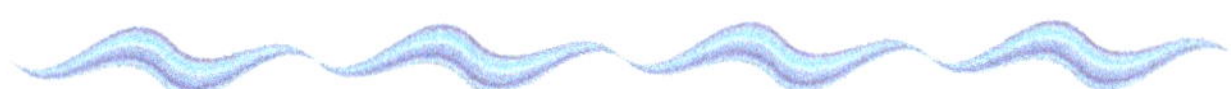

Marlette Lake Looking Northwest

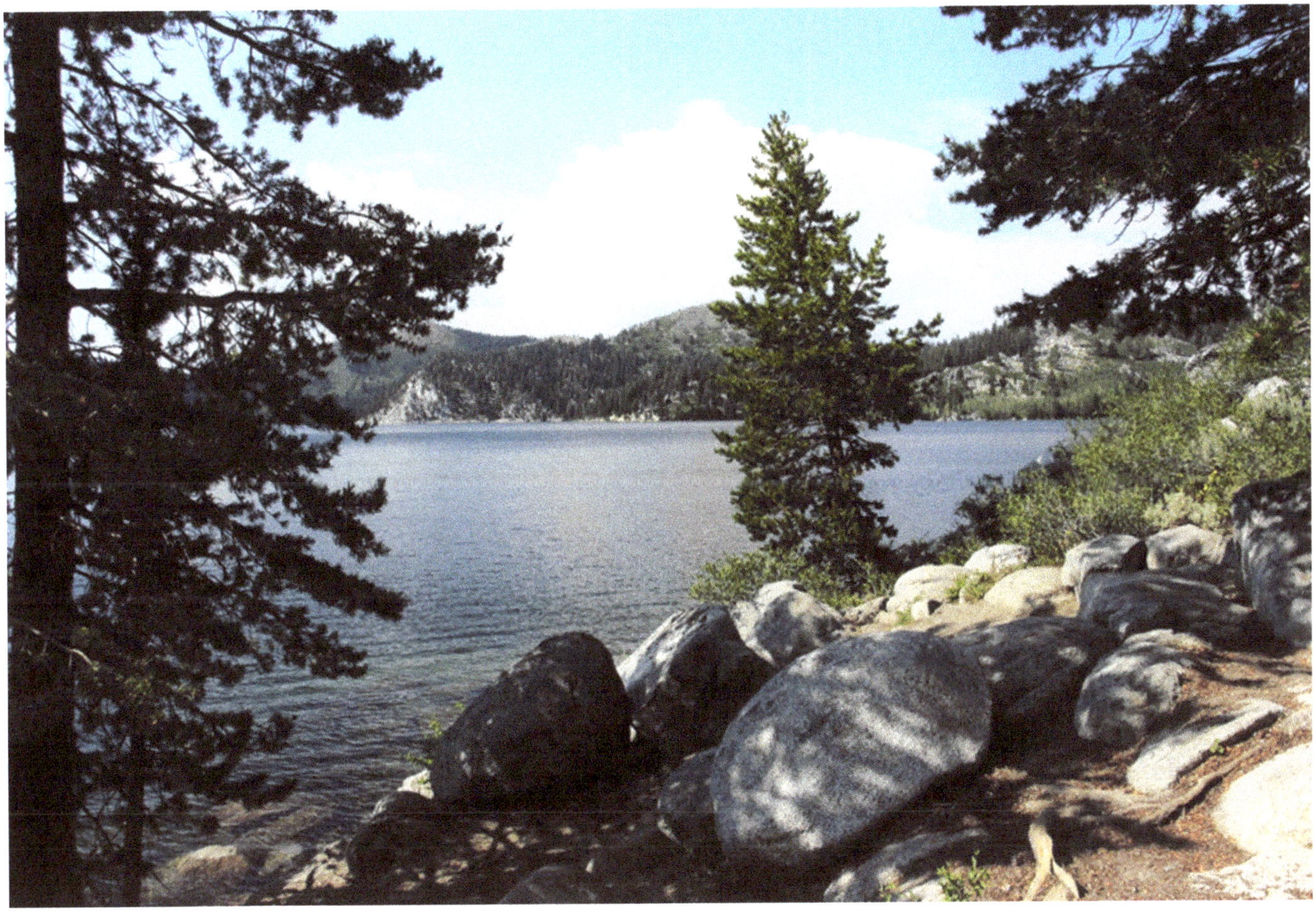

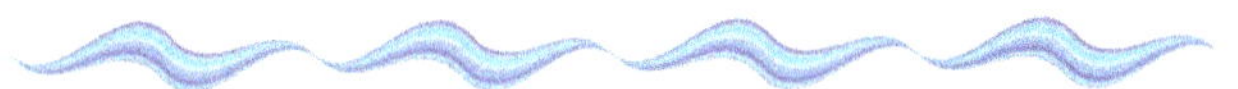

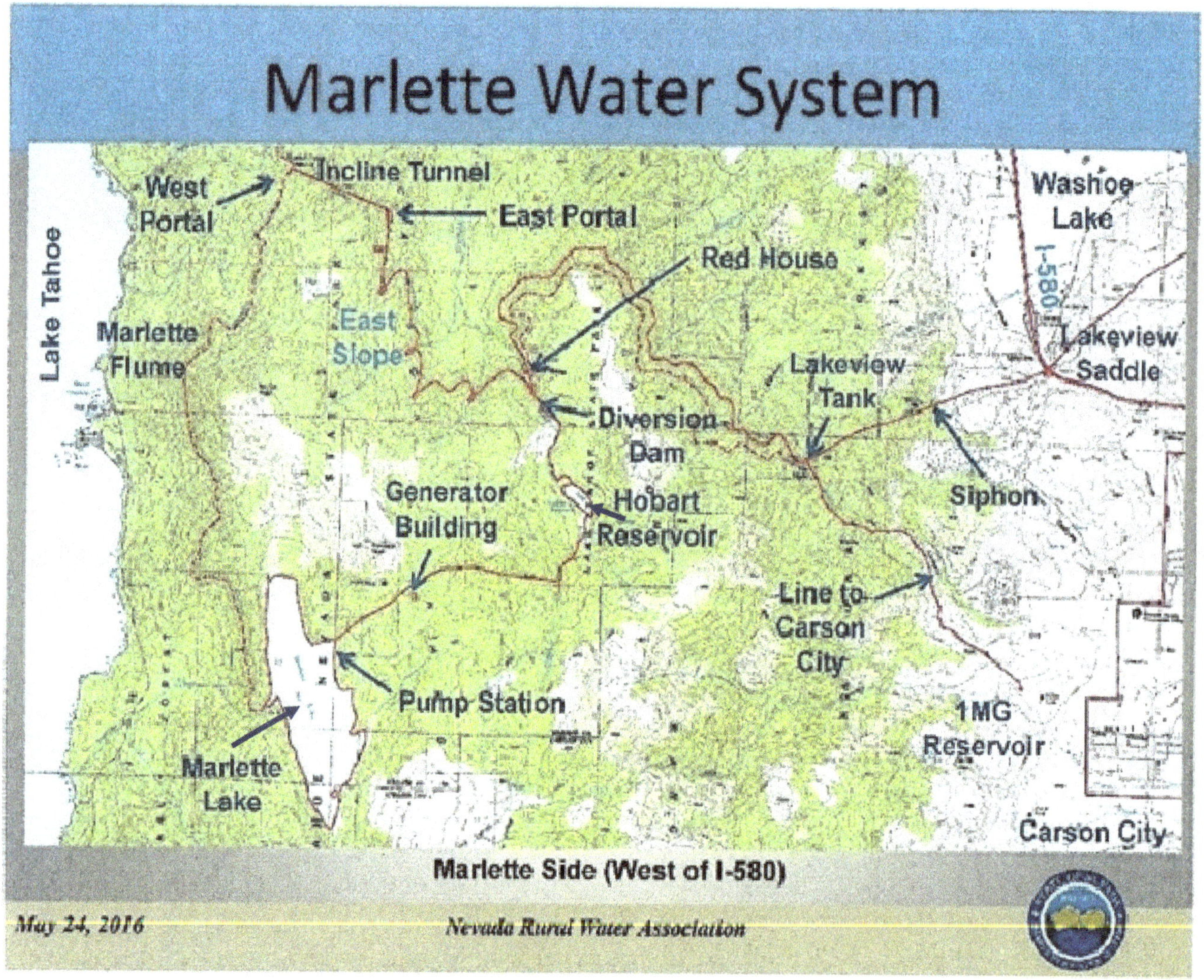

Marlette Water System

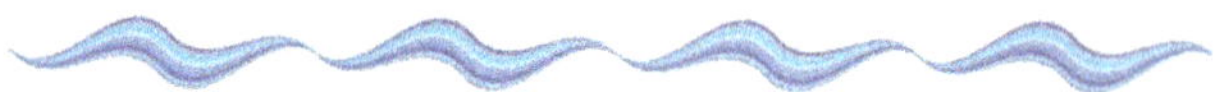

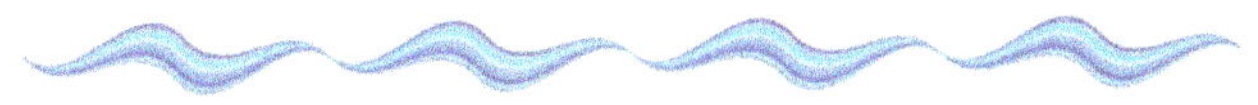

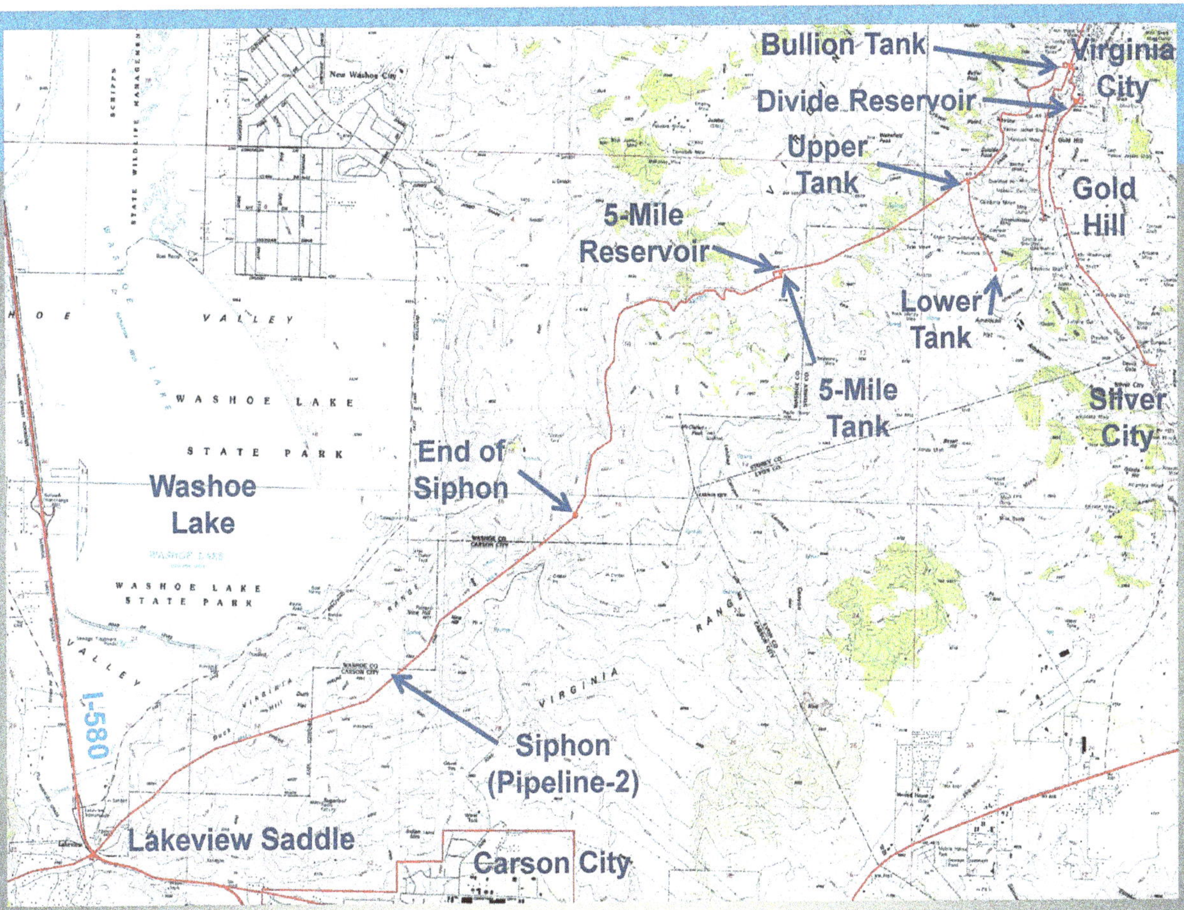

Storey County Side (East of I-580)

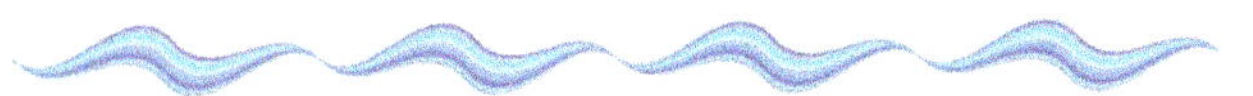

May 24, 2016

Nevada Rural Water Association

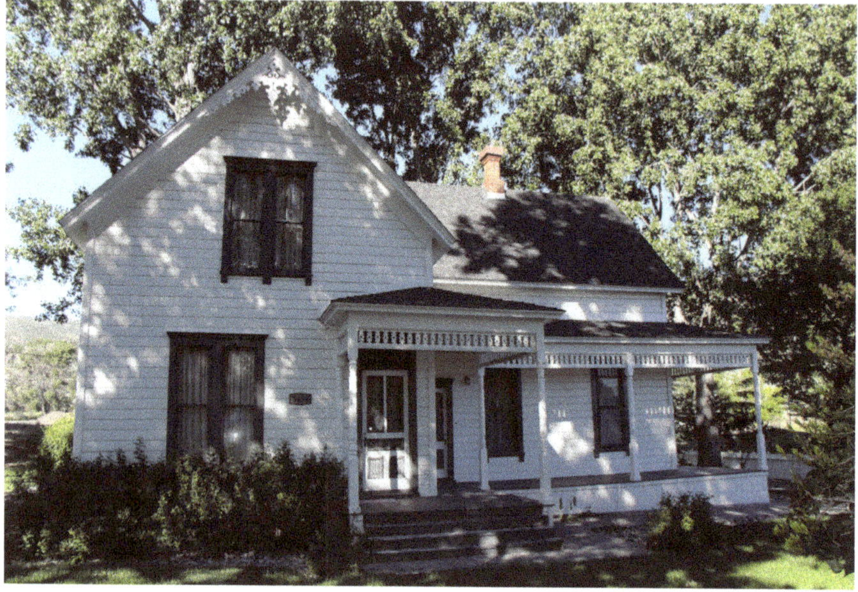

The Water Masters House. The house was built in 1873 at Lakeview

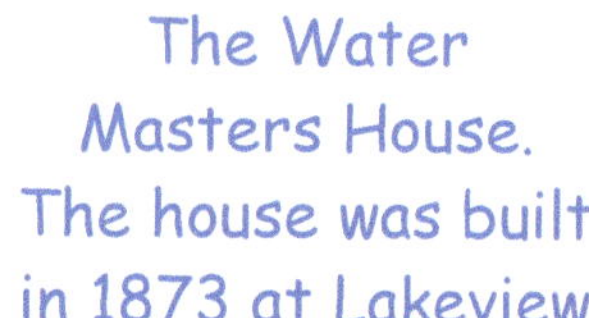

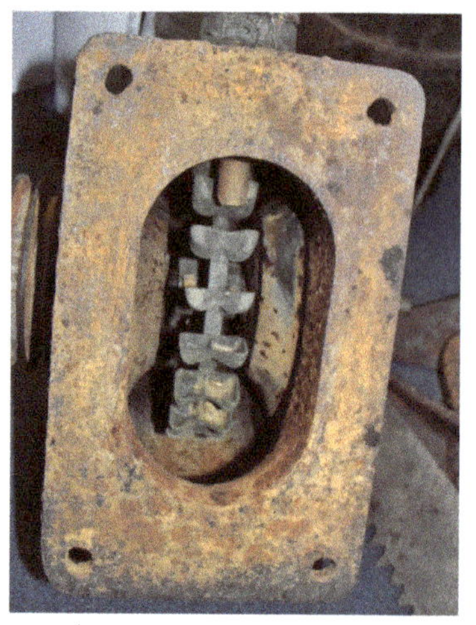

- The pipeline came down the mountain and ran under the Water Masters House.
- The Pelton Wheel pictured here (located in the basement), provided power to run the electric generator for the house.

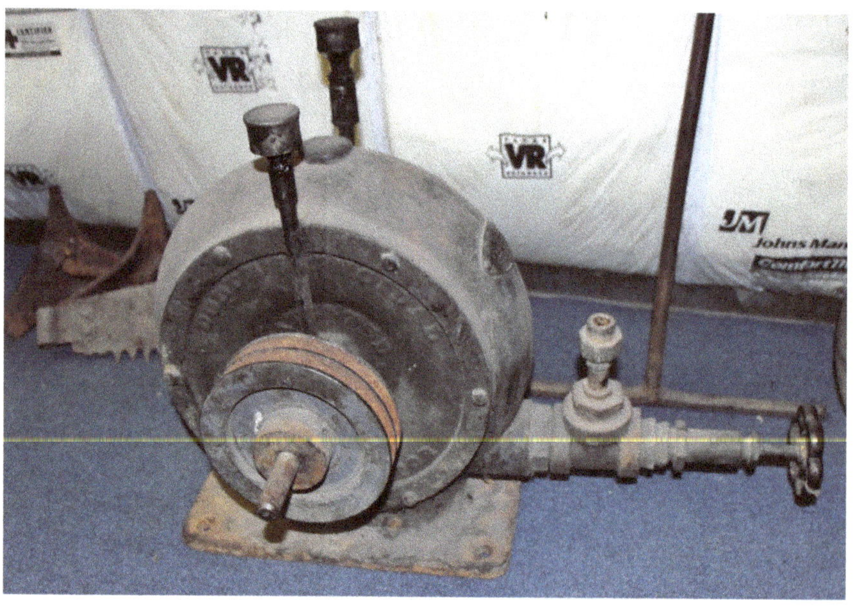

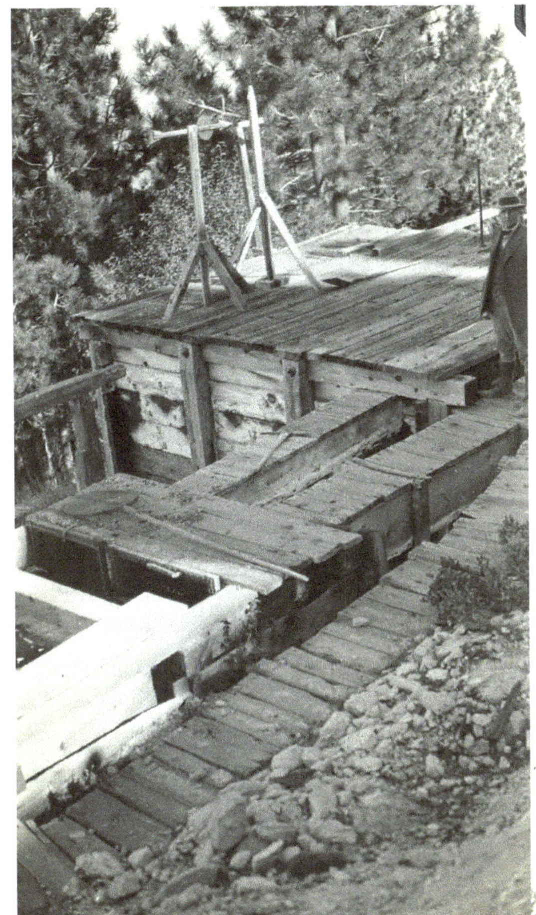

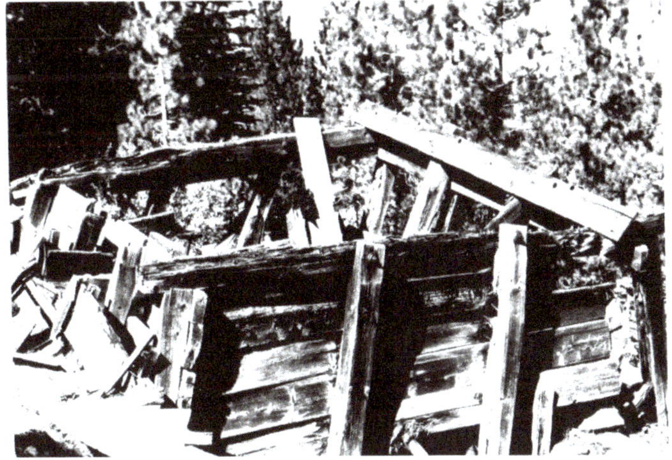

The square tank provided water to the caretakers Tank House pictured on the left. There were two other tanks that held the water for the Virginia City area.

The operators who would control the slide gates for water demand on the Comstock lived in the Tank House.

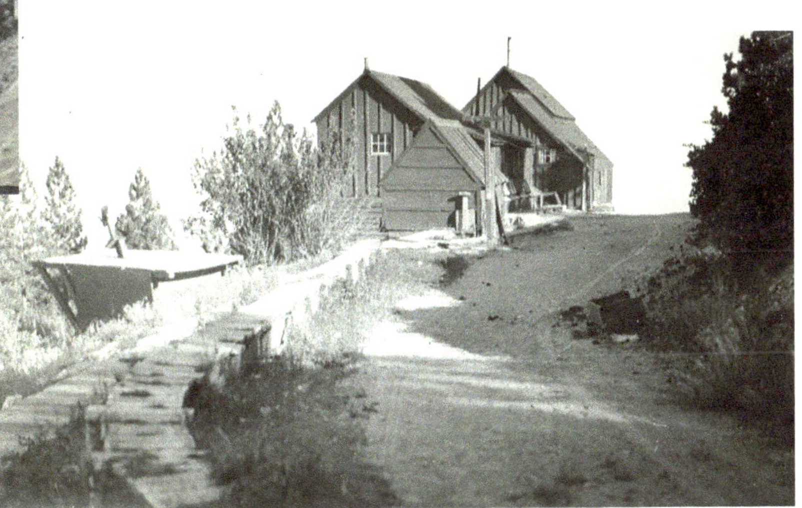

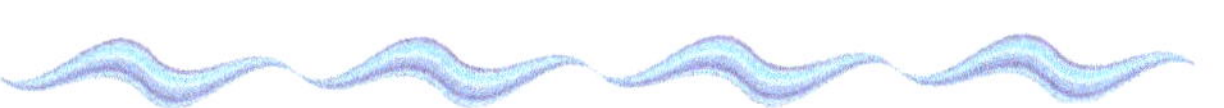

Tank House

The old wooden tanks at Lakeview. These tanks were burned in 1981.

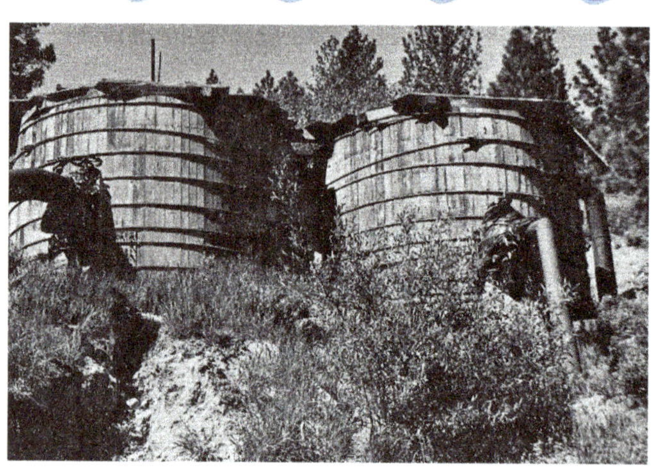

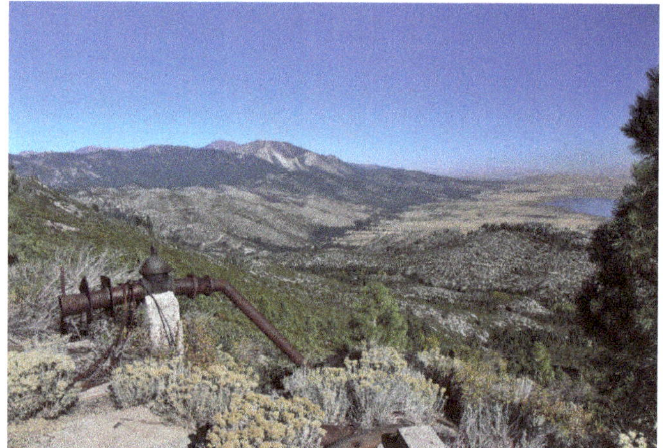

Valve connectors for the old redwood tanks. View of Slide Mountain from the Lakeview Tanks.

From here the water was diverted to Virginia City and Carson City. This is the current tank and holds 22,000 gallons of water.

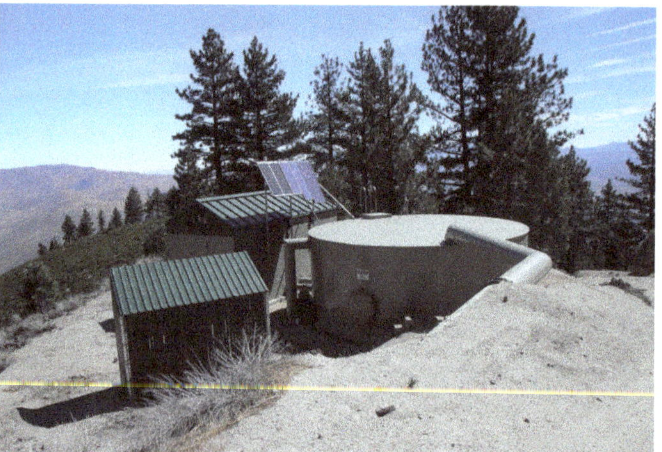

Lakeview storage tank that replaced the burned wooden tanks

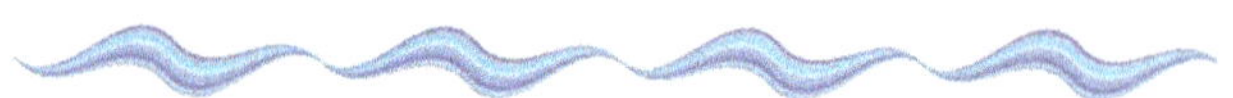

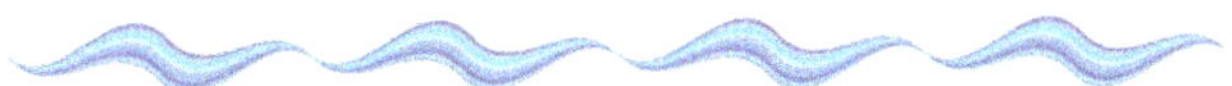

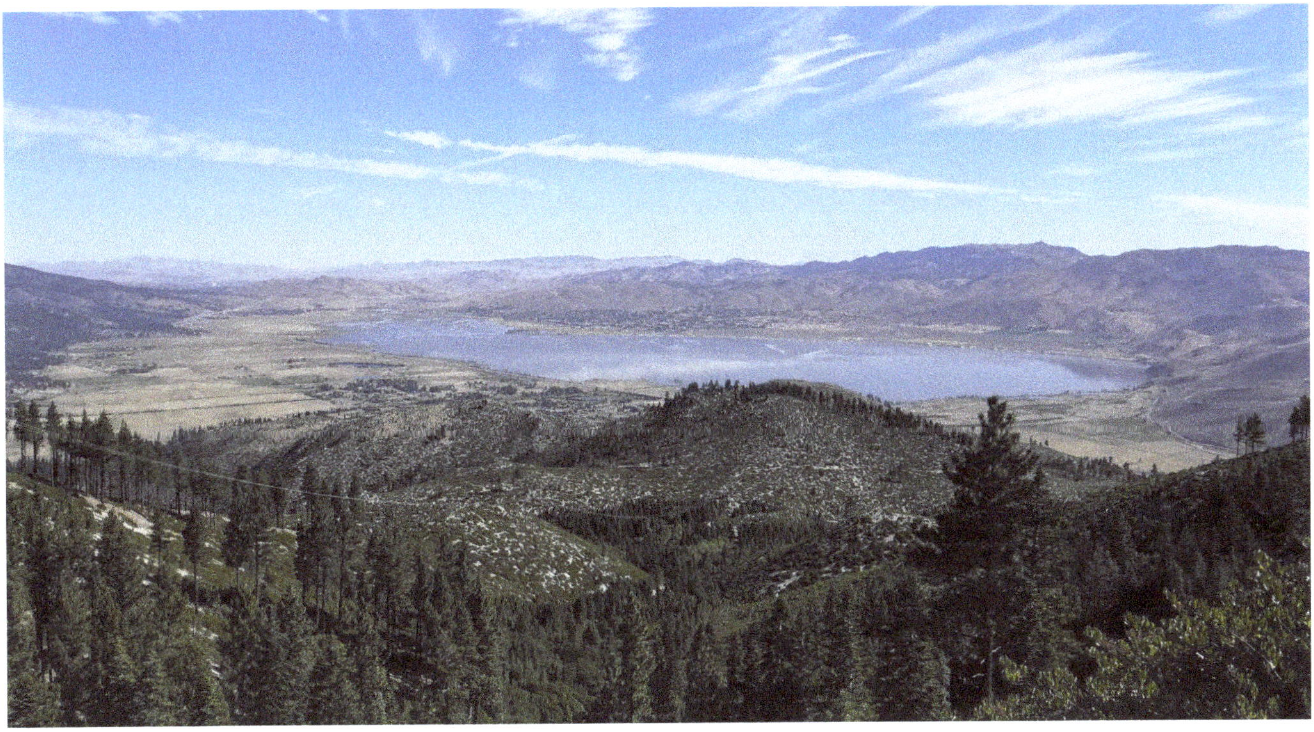

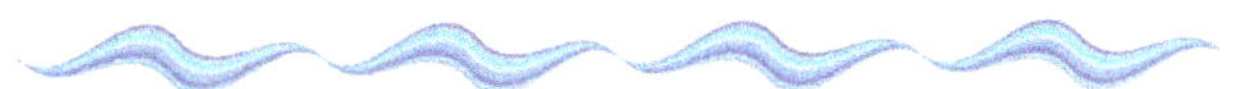

The view of Washoe Lake from the top of the mountain.

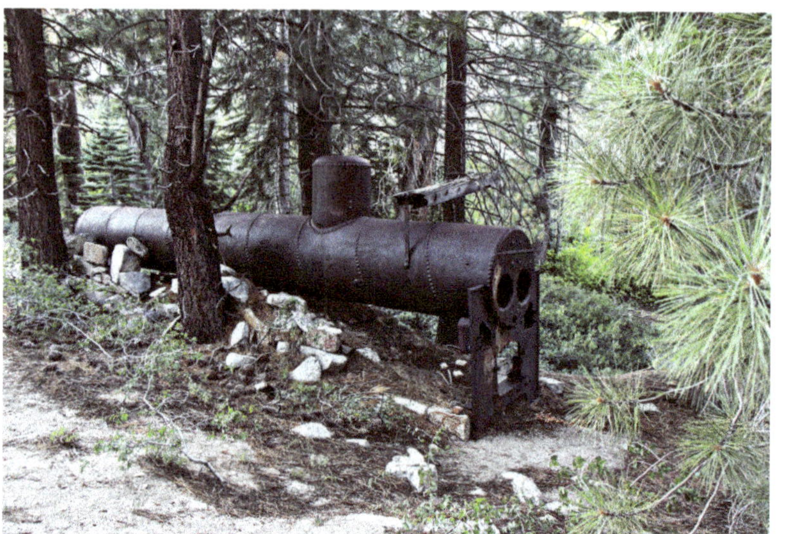

Sawmill Canyon
Steam boiler for steam
powered sawmill

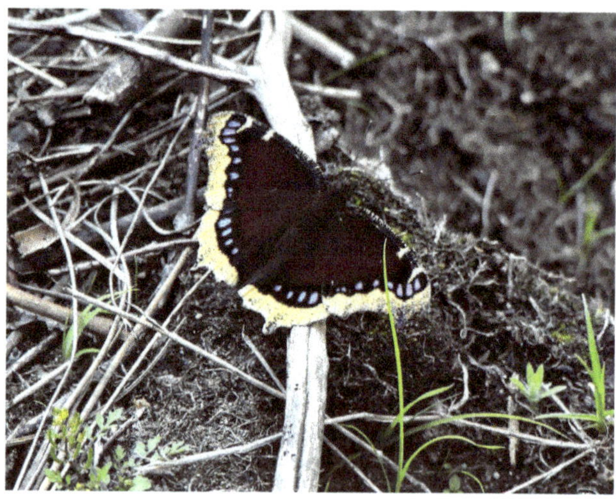

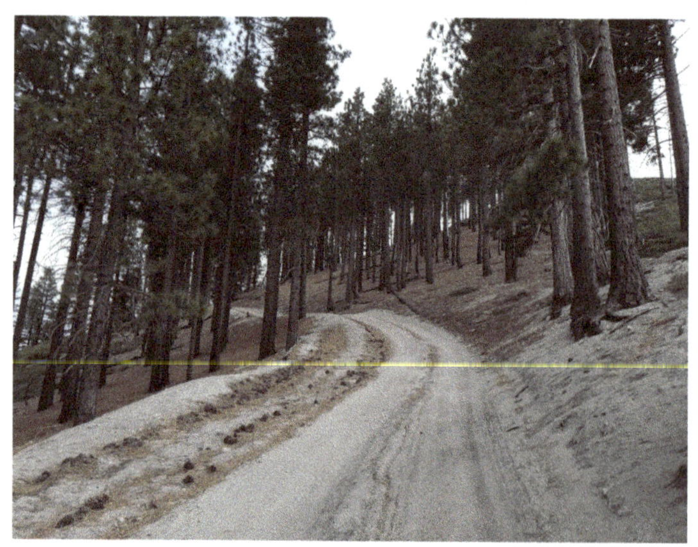

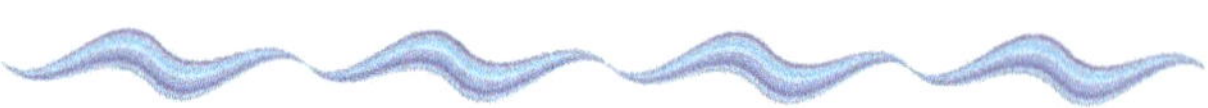

The road up the mountain

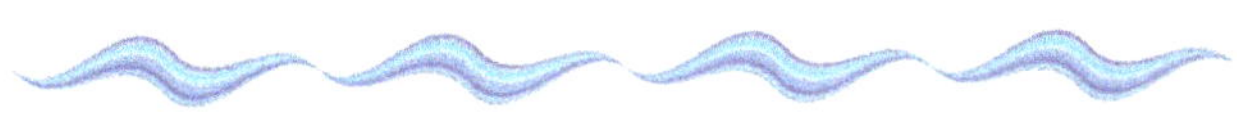

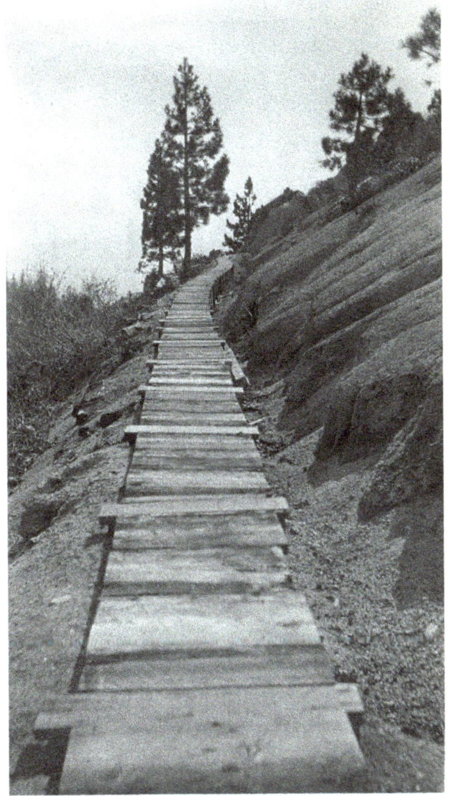

Marlette Flume

Marlette Flume
- Built in 1877
- 4.38 miles long from Marlette Lake to the West Portal of the Incline Tunnel

- North Flume, also known as the "Incline Flume".
- 8.23 miles long from Incline to West Portal.
- Collected water from the many creeks on the west side of the mountain.

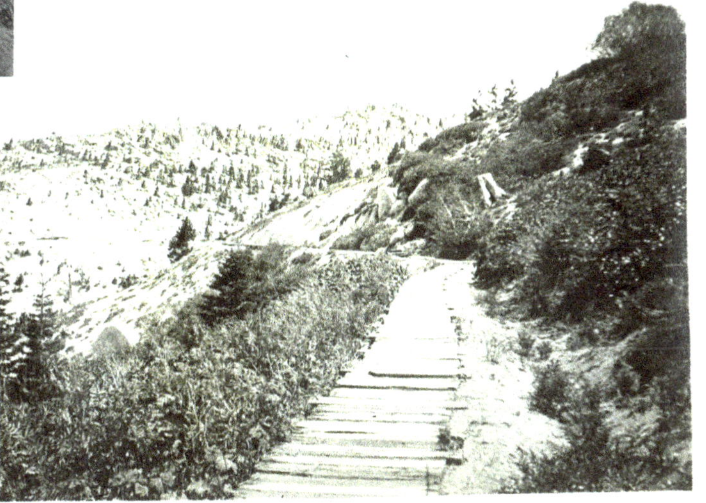

North Flume

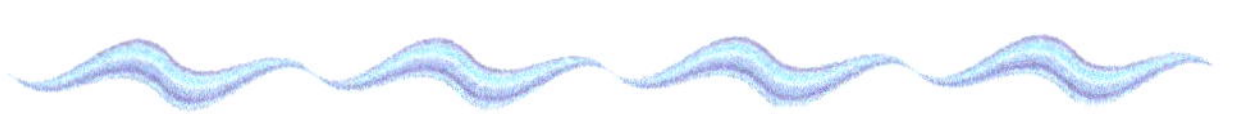

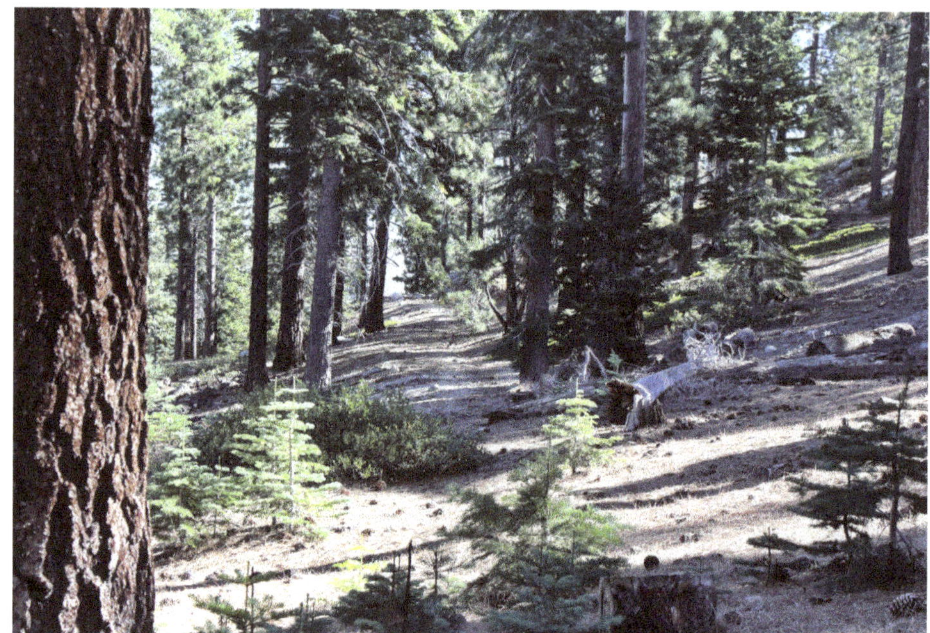

Remnants of the upper
wooden water flume

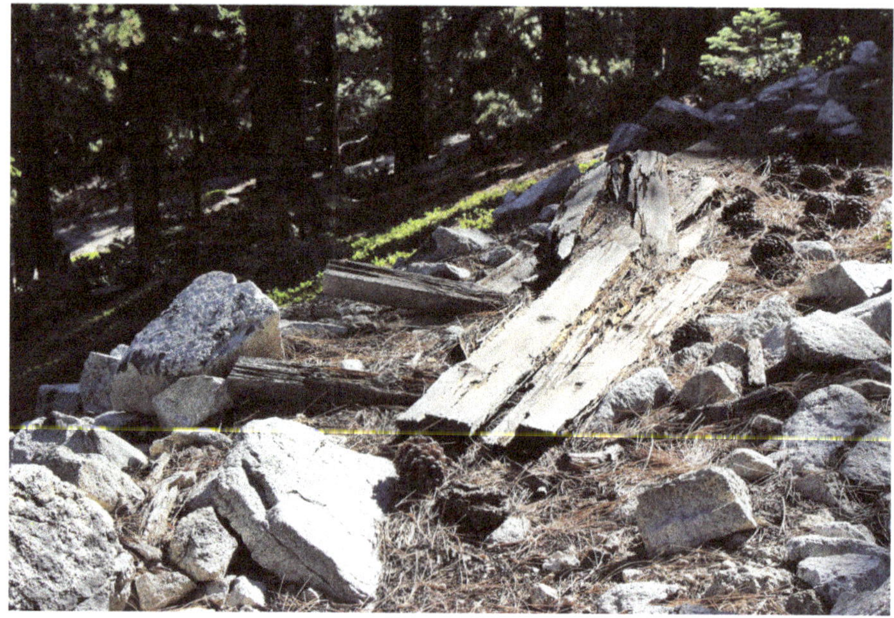

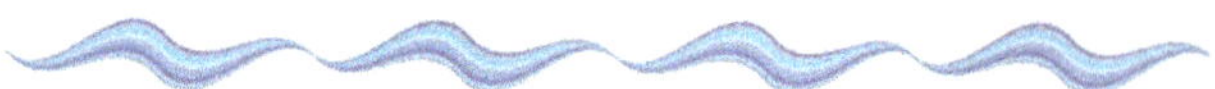

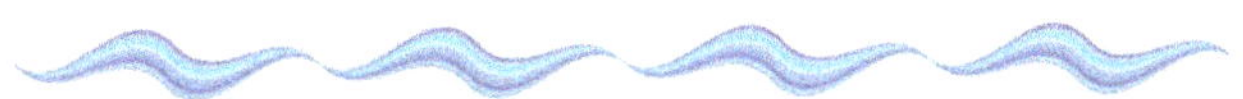

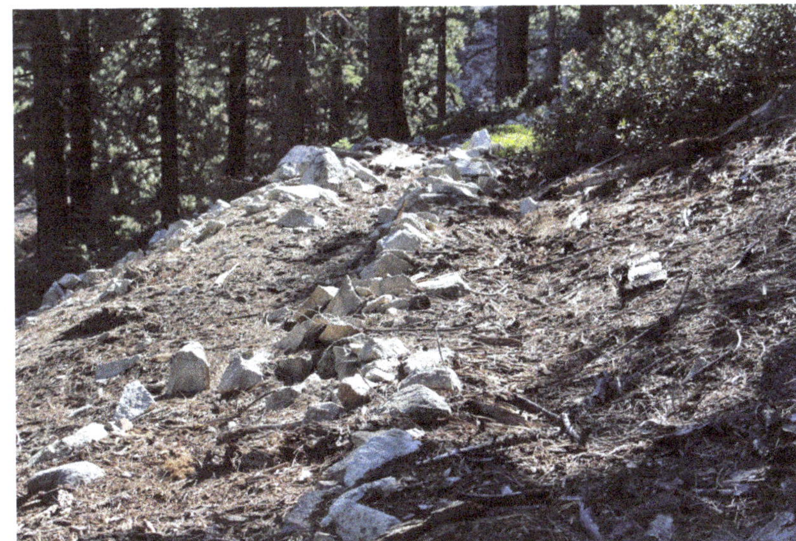

More remnants of the upper
wooden water flume

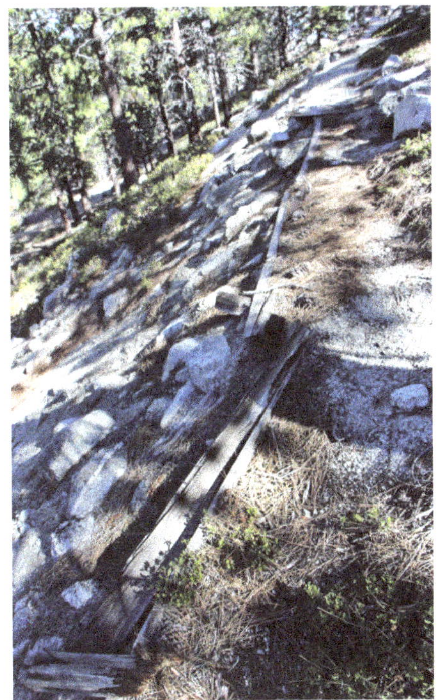

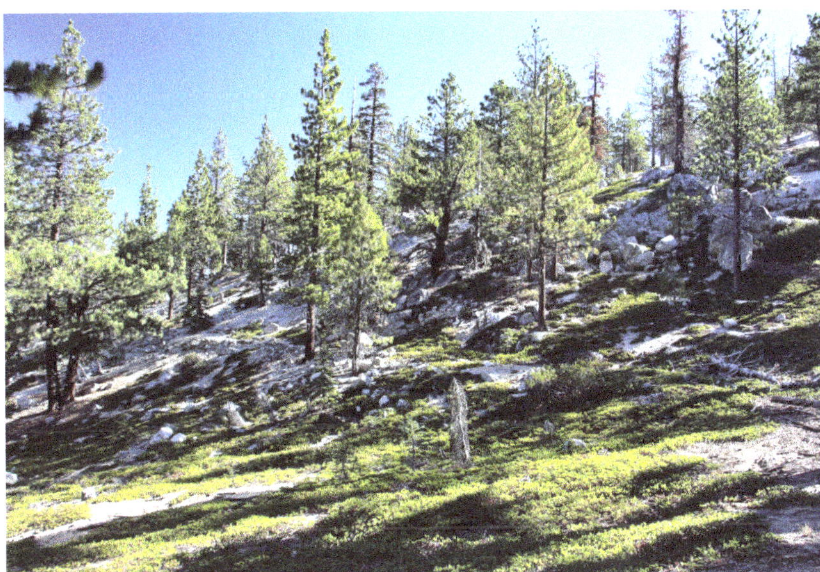

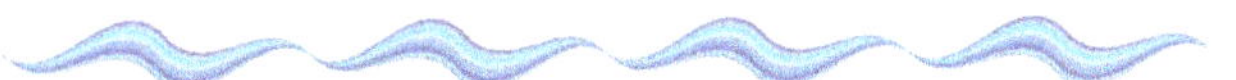

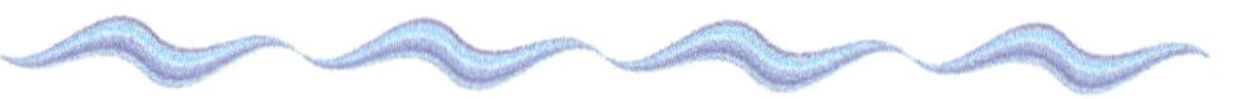

Walter S. Hobart, who partnered with Seneca Hunt Marlette, was a lumber man with logging interests and involved in the water flume.

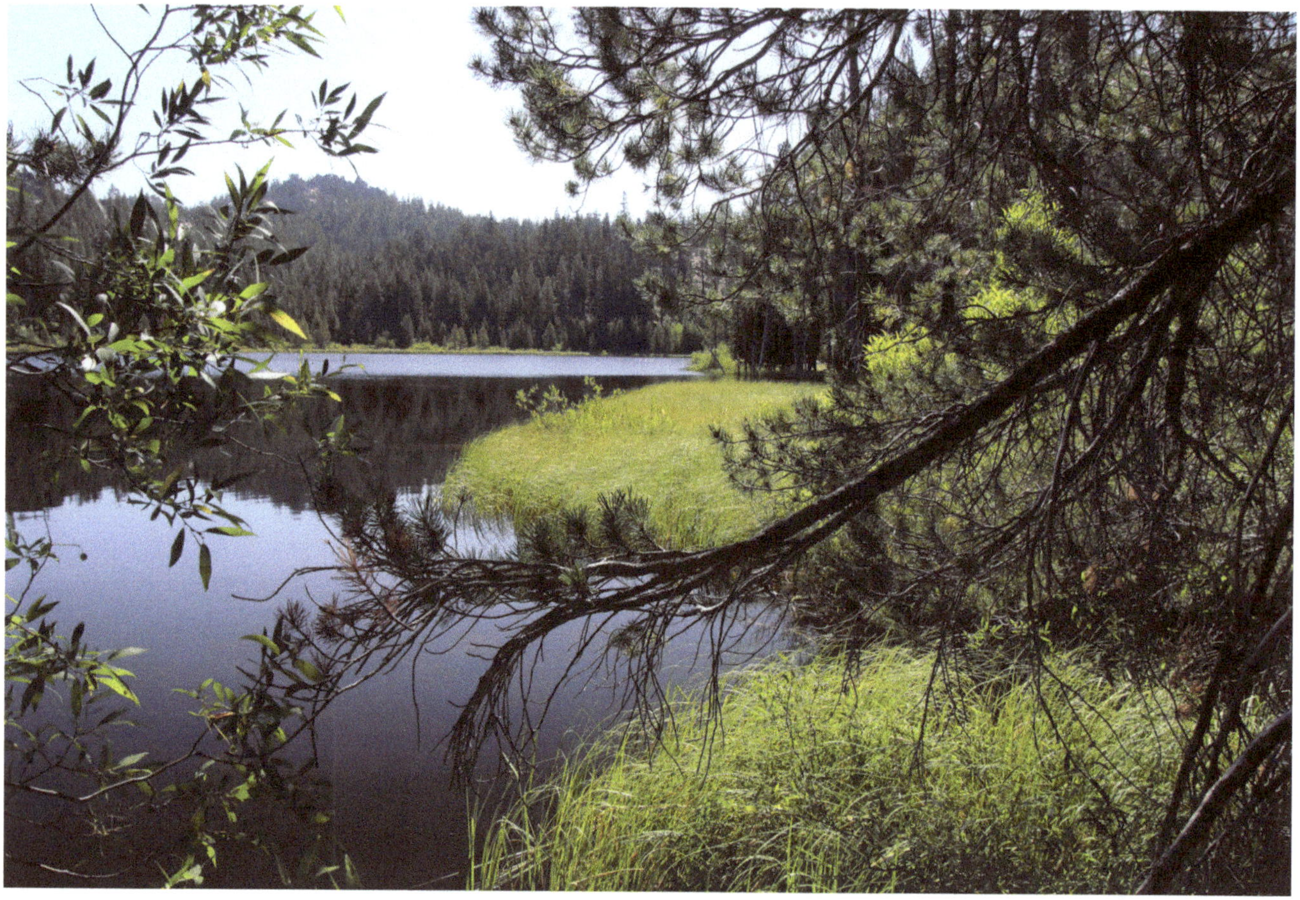

Hobart Creek Reservoir (looking south), named after Waler S. Hobart, was originally built in 1877.

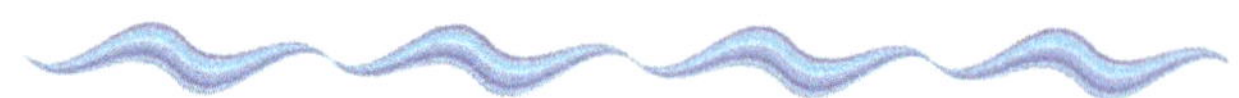

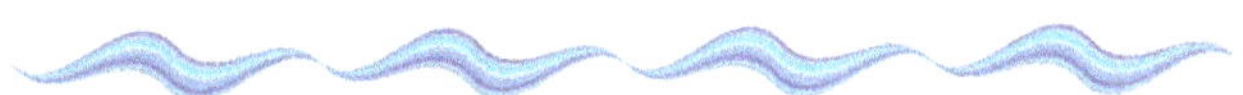

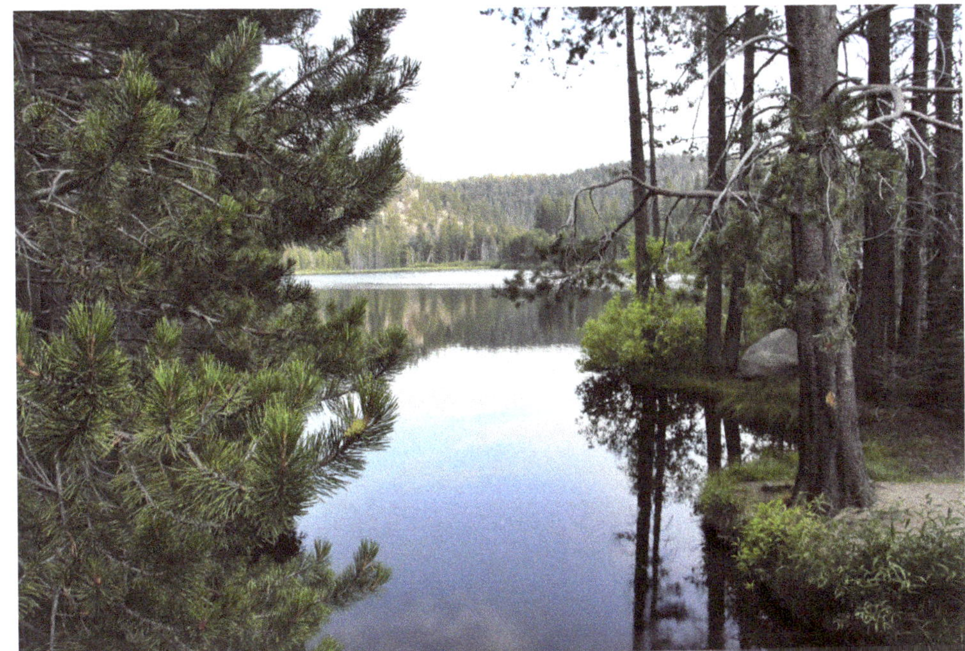

Views of Hobart
Creek Reservoir

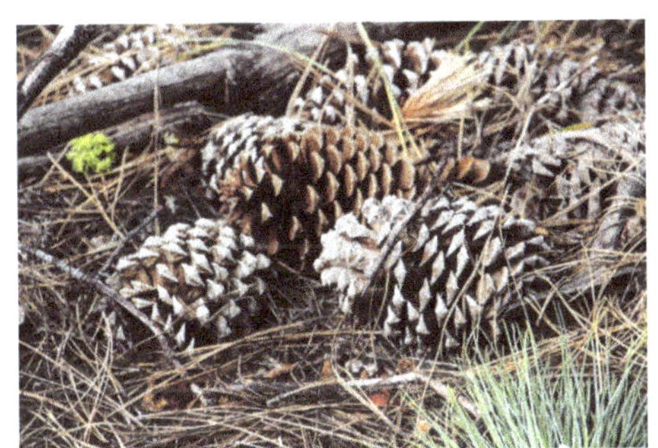

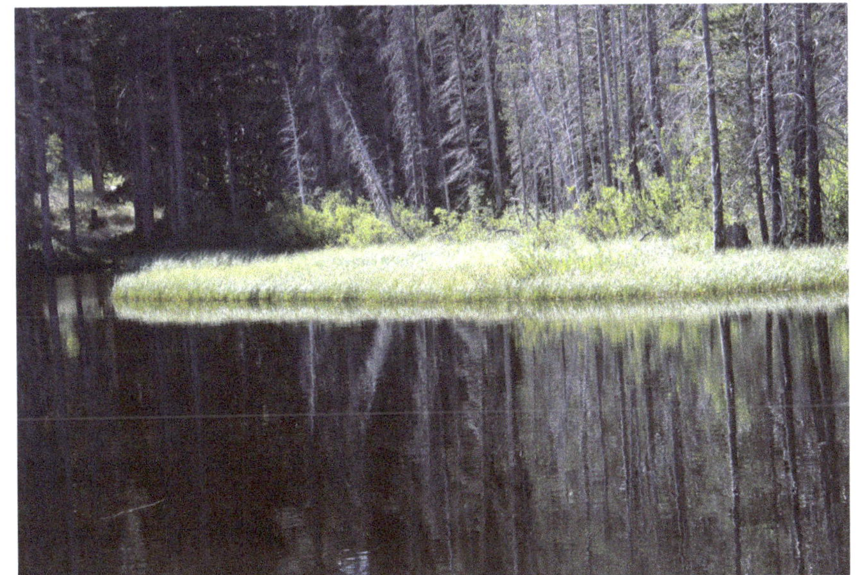

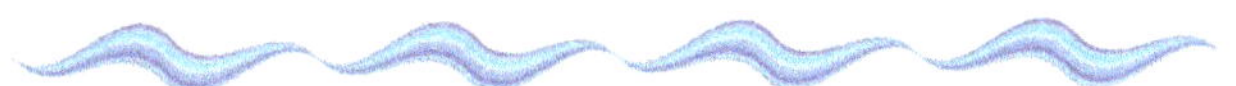

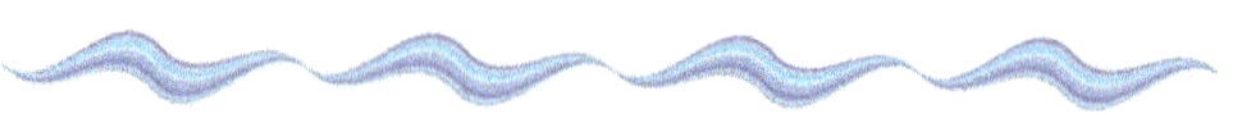

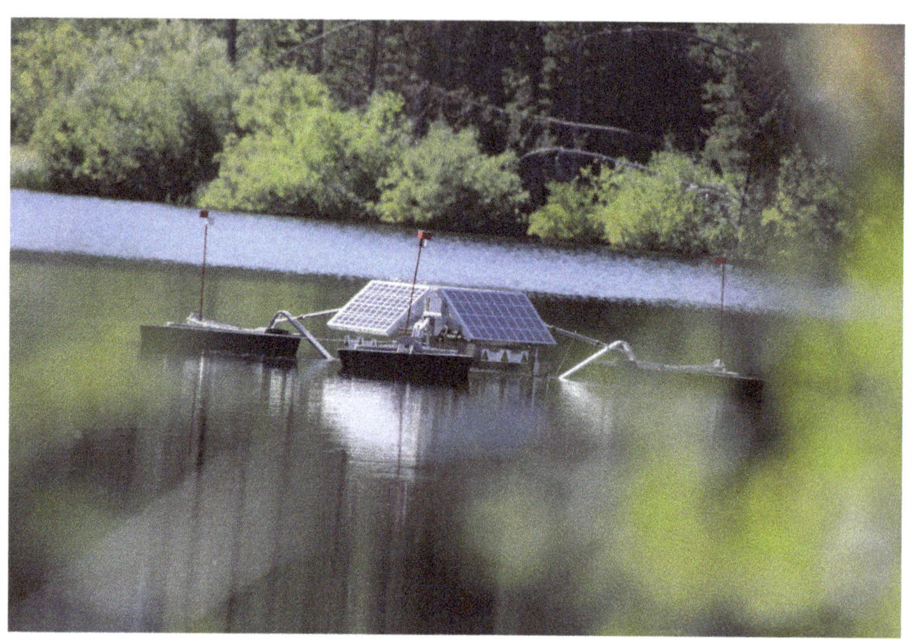

Solar Bee Water Recirculator to purify the water at Hobart Creek Reservoir

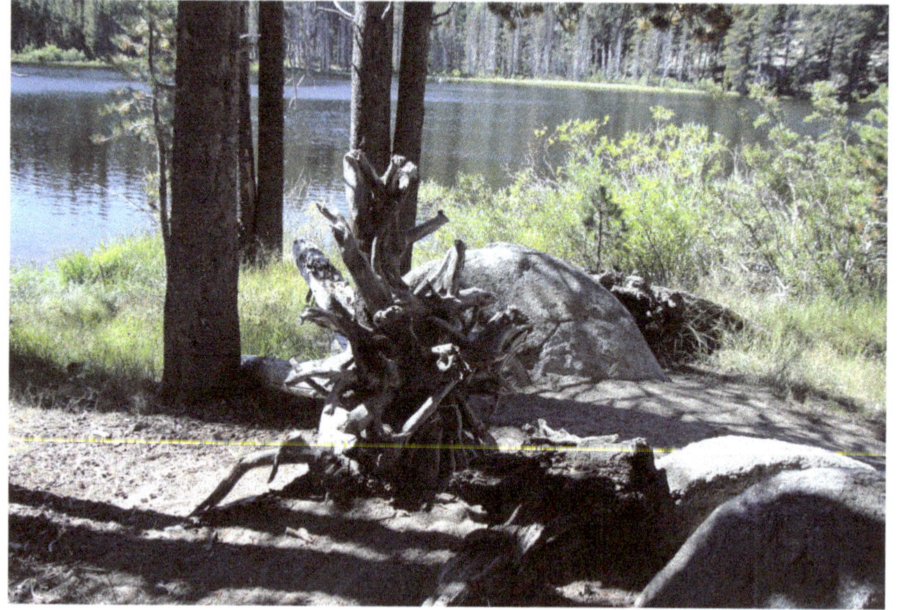

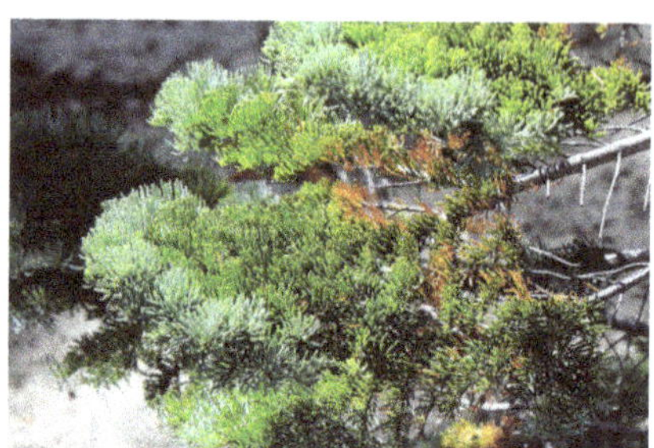

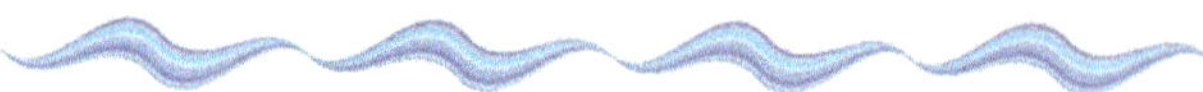

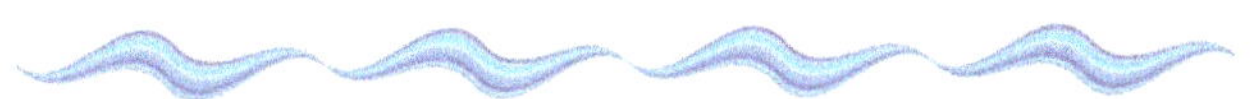

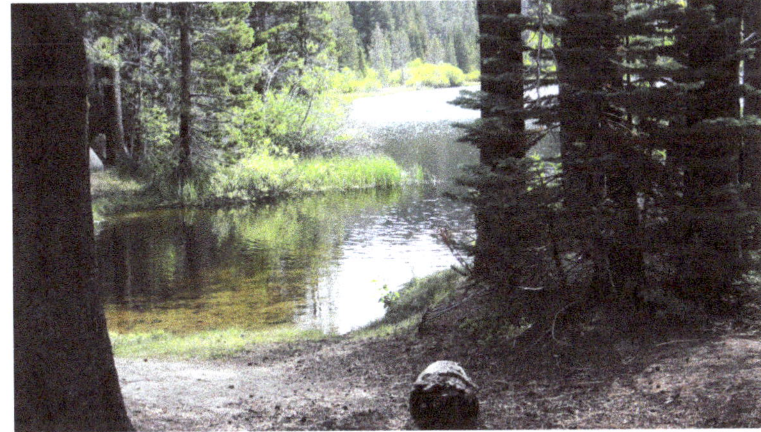

Water going into
Hobart Creek

Bridge over Hobart Creek

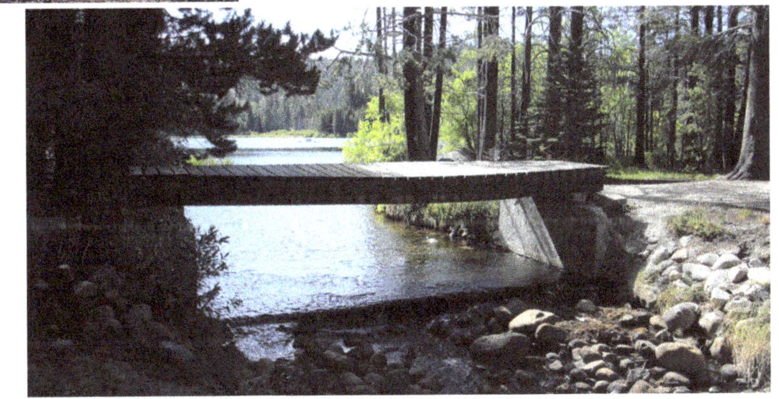

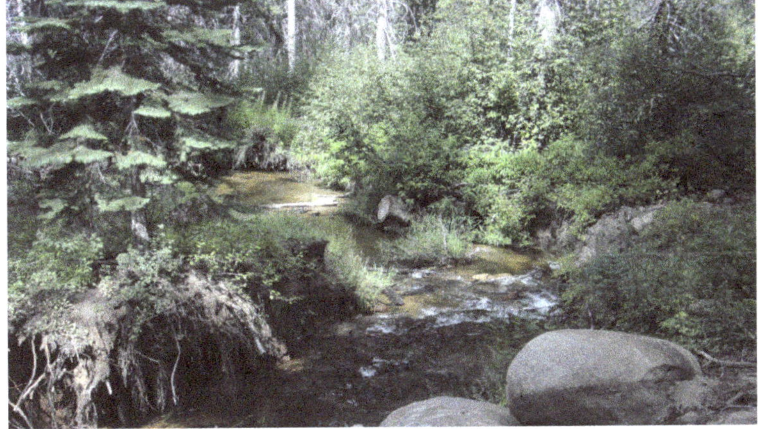

Hobart Creek

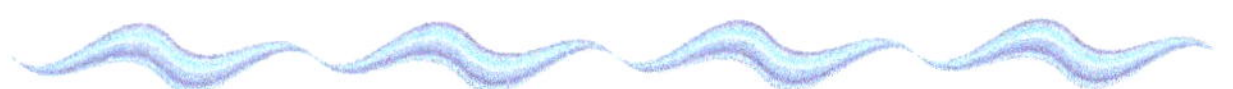

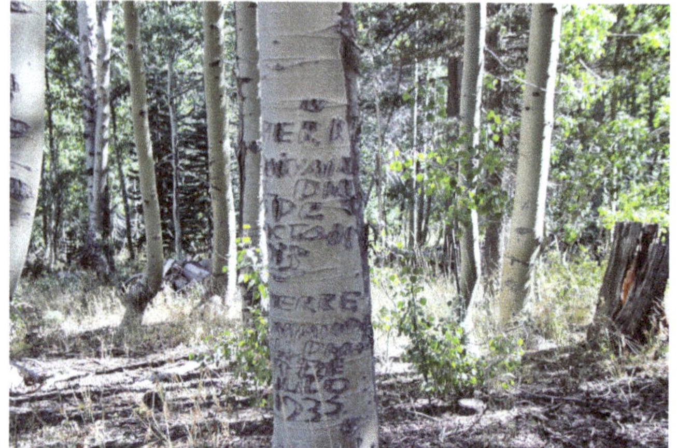
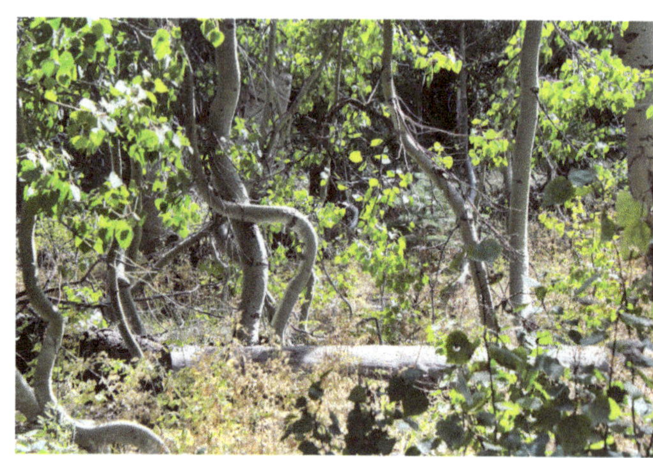

Aspen grove with Basque carvings

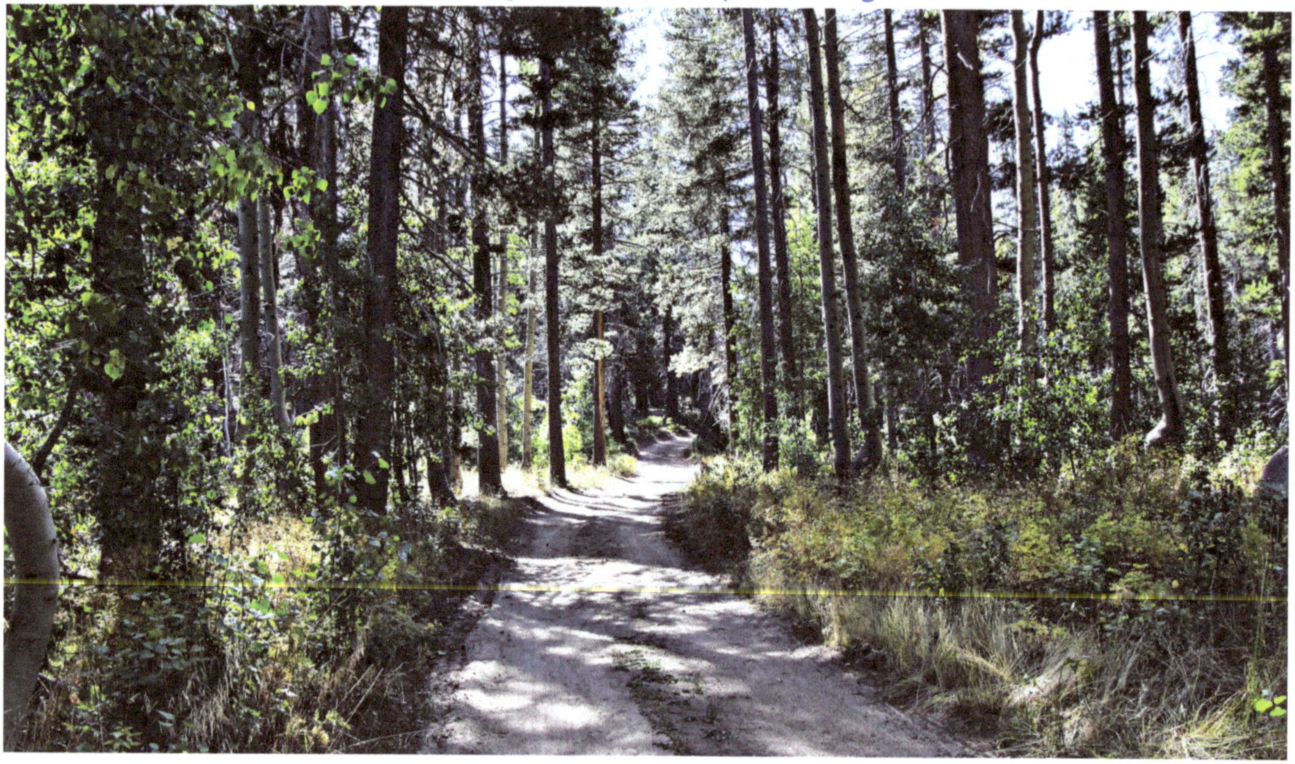

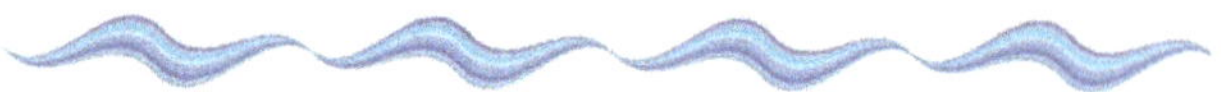

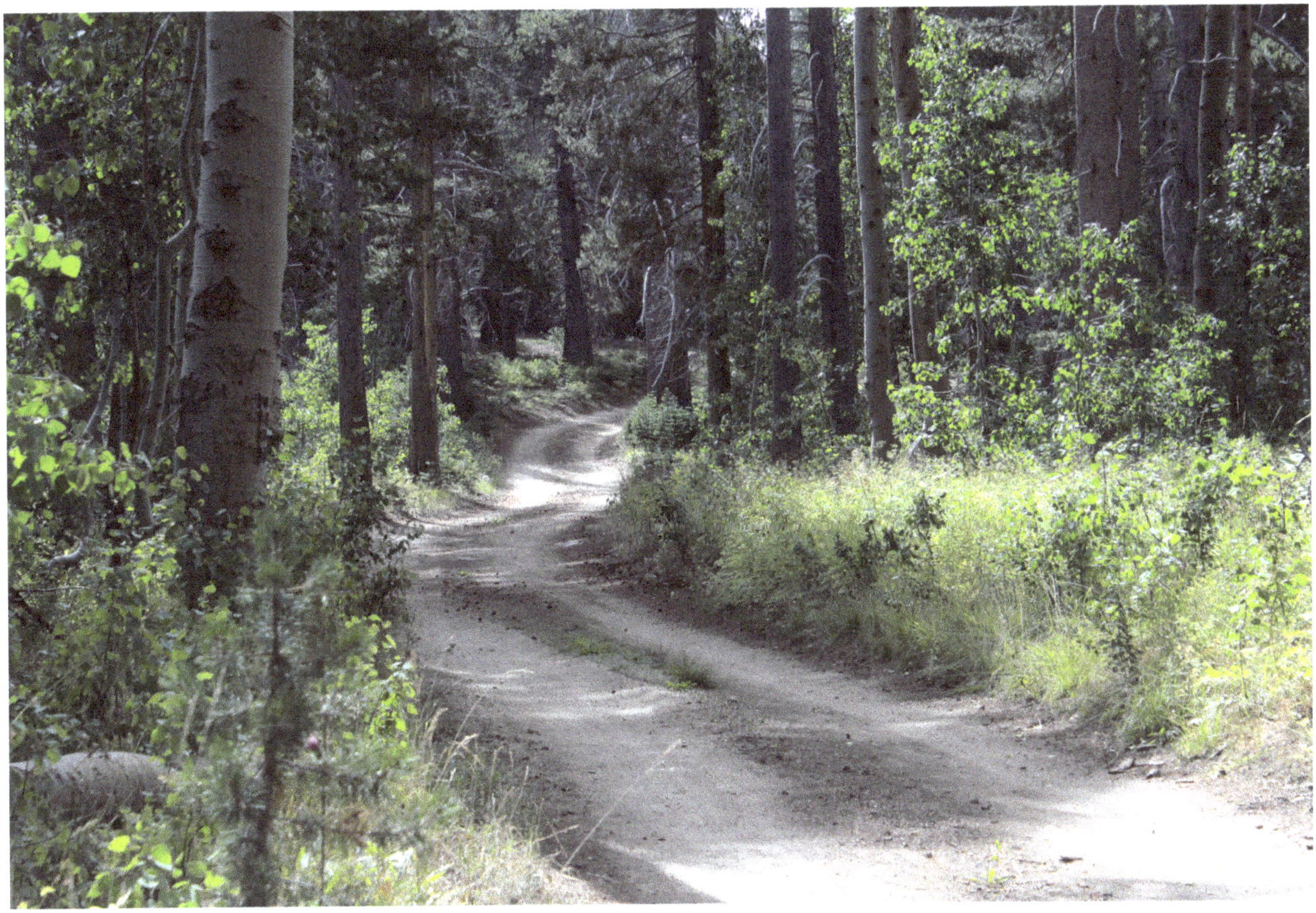

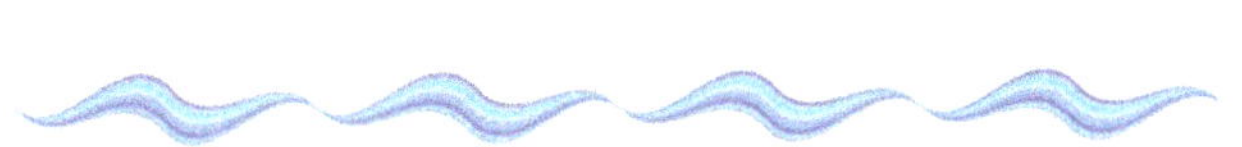

Another beautiful road in the Hobart/Marlette Lake area

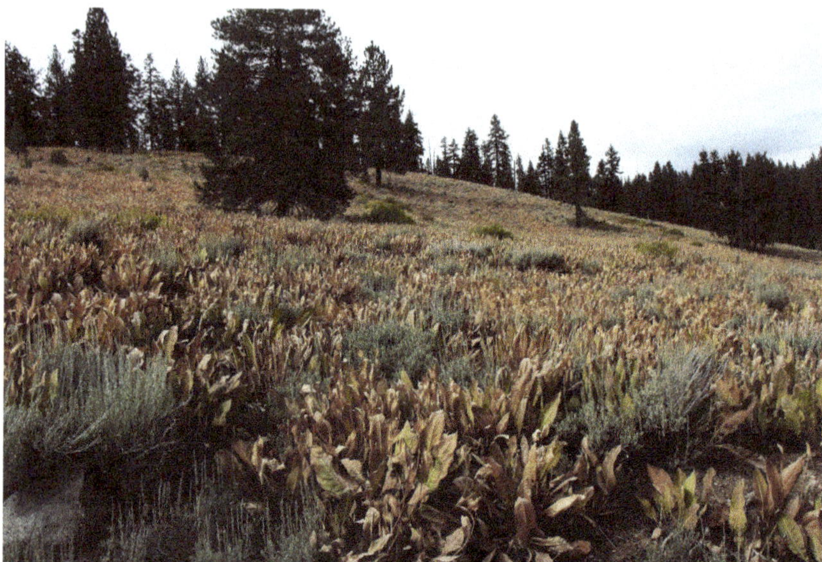

On the road to
Marlette Lake

Field of Mule Ears plants

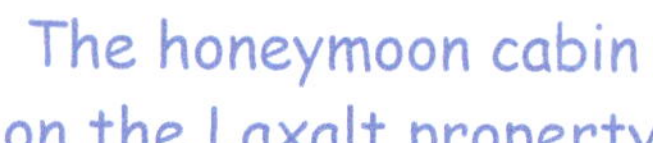

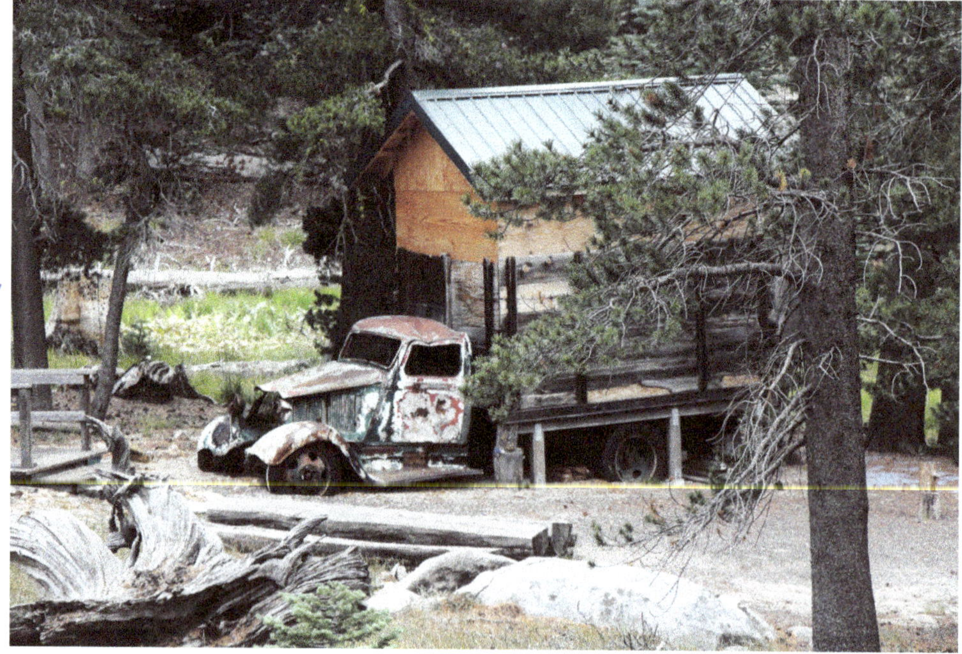

The honeymoon cabin
on the Laxalt property

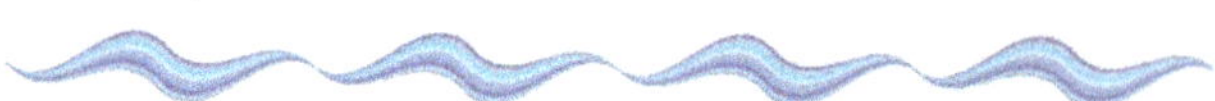

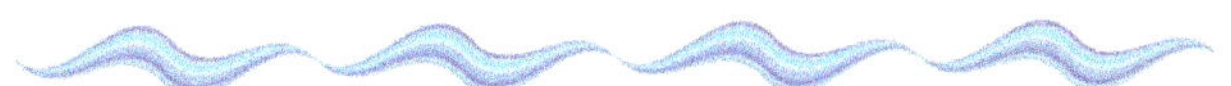

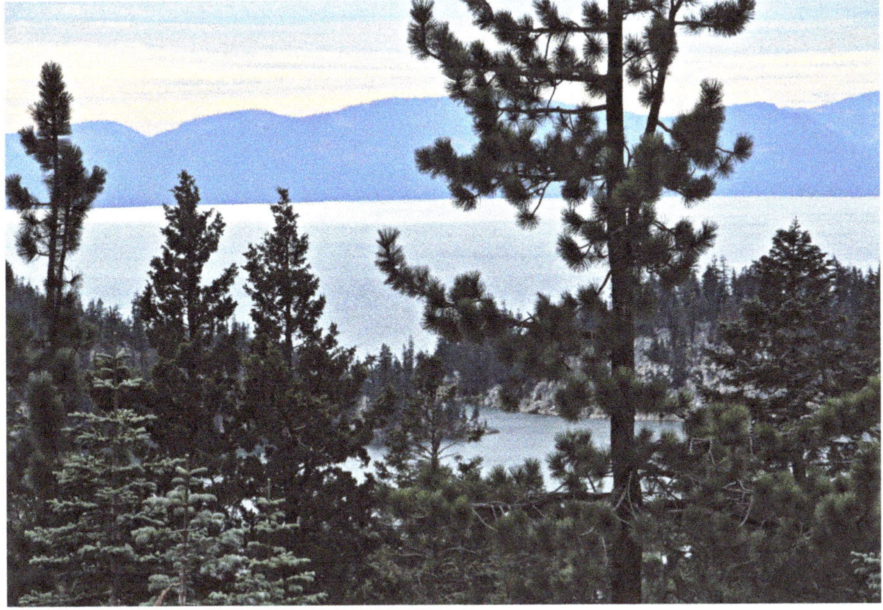

Marlette Lake with Lake Tahoe in the background

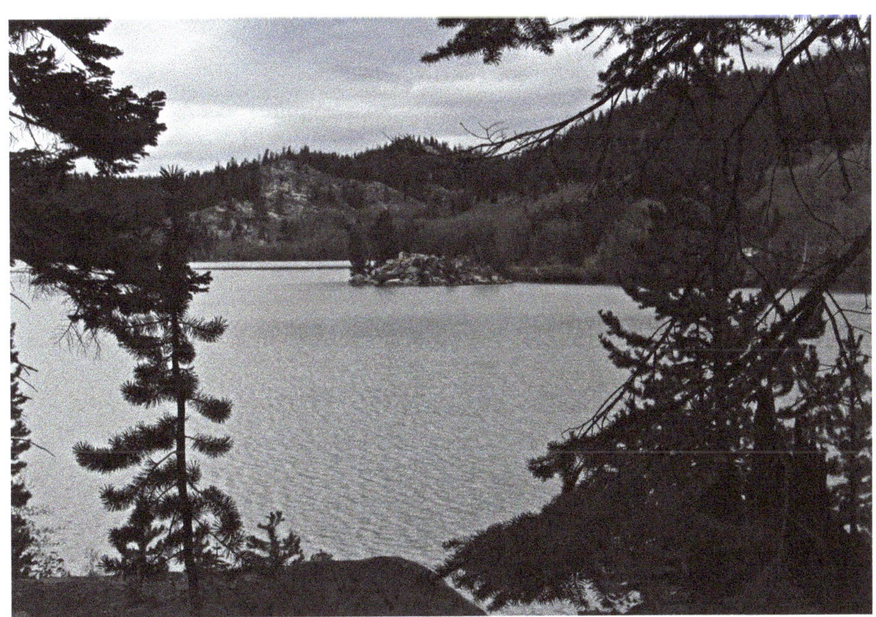

Marlette Lake named after Seneca Hunt Marlette, Civil Engineer, was the first Surveyor General in Nevada.

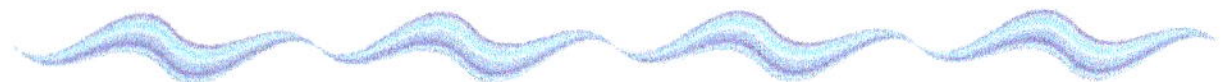

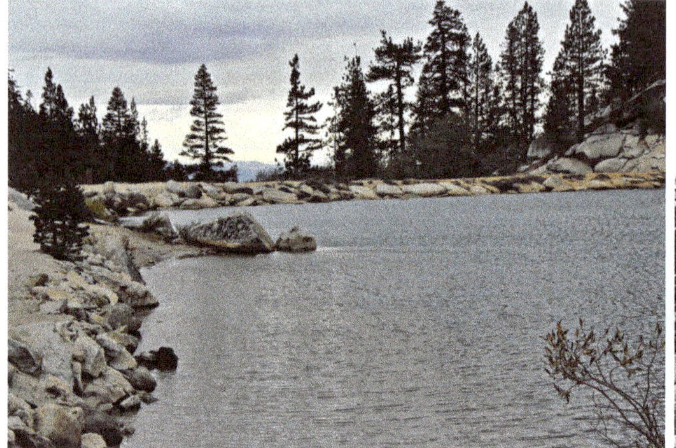

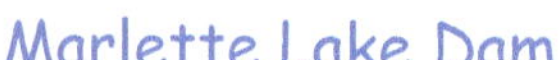

Marlette Lake Dam

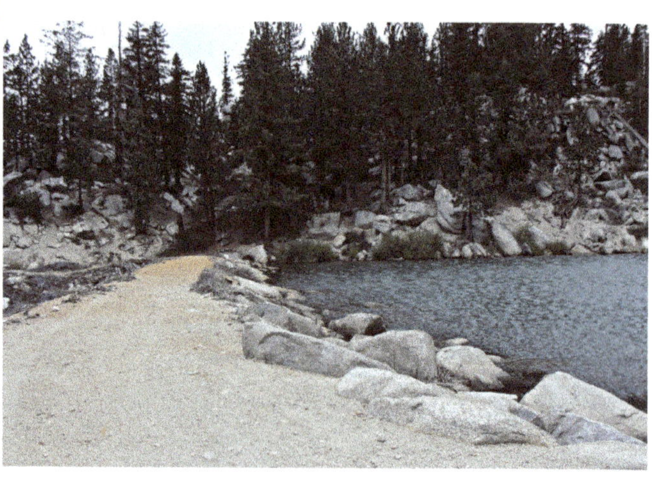

Looking at Marlette
Lake from the dam

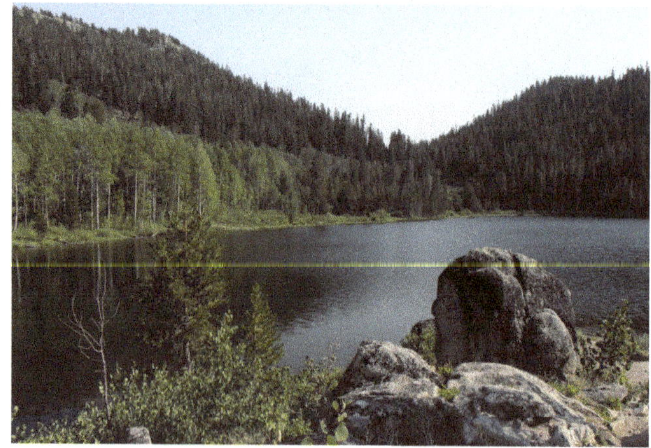

Marlette Lake was first created
as a lake for logging operations
by the Elliot Brothers in 1868.

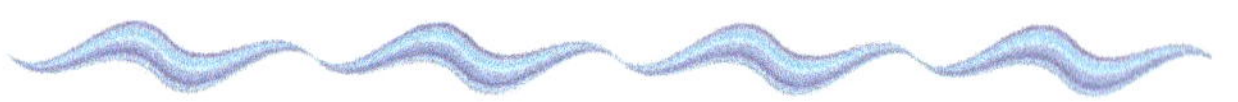

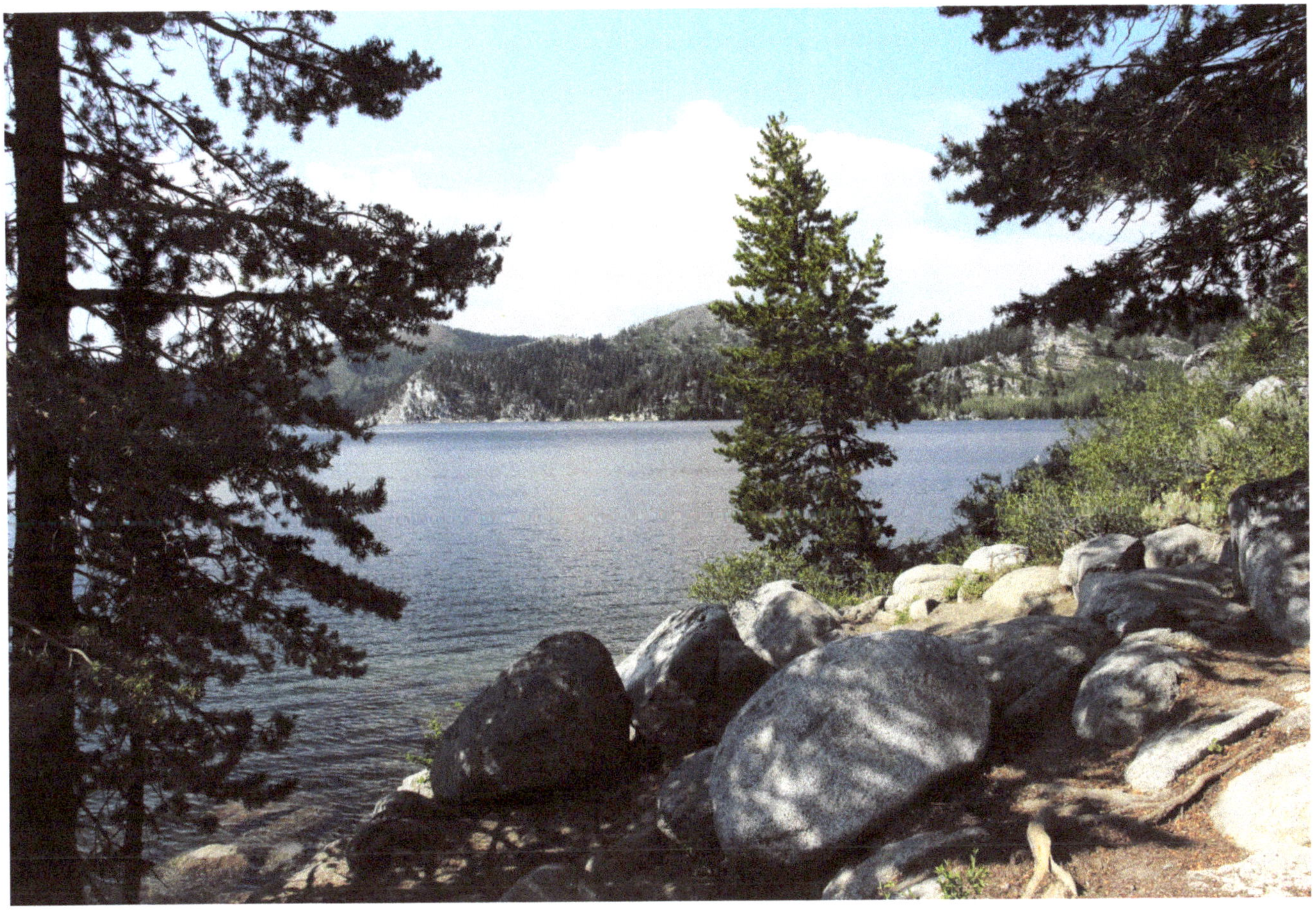

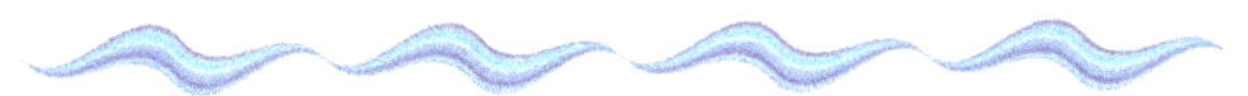

Marlette Lake looking to the west

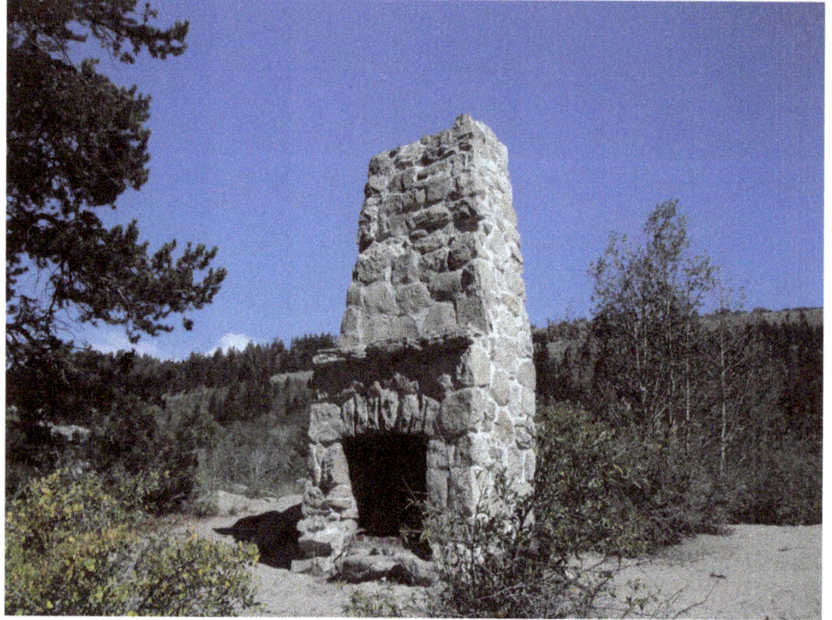

In 1933 James and Jessie Leonard acquired the Virginia and Gold Hill Water Company. They changed the name to Virginia City Water Company and built a recreational cabin on the site known as Chimney Point. In 1963 the State of Nevada purchased the water company.

In the late 1960's the state sent a crew to tear down the caretakers cabin near the dam. The crew demolished the Leonard cabin by mistake. All that remains is the chimney.

The caretakers house at Marlette Dam (1868) was maintained by Virginia and Gold Hill Water Company. Similar caretakers residents were built at the west portal of the tunnel, such as, Red House Diversion Dam, Tank House and Five Mile Reservoir.

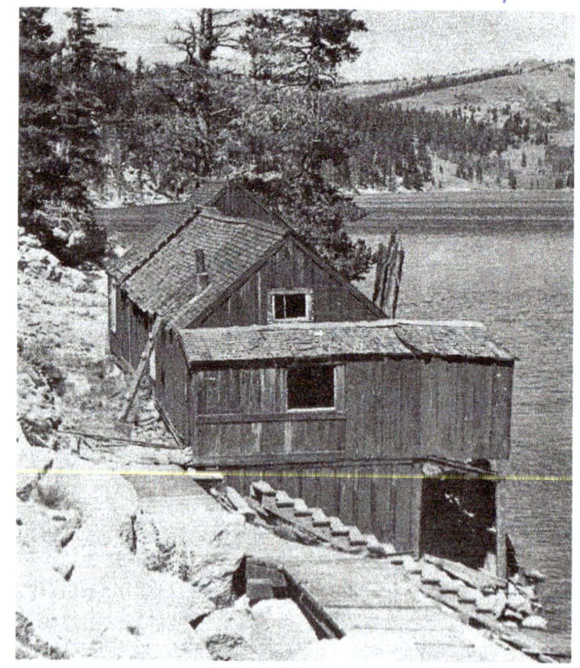

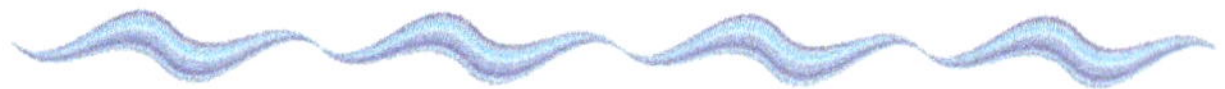

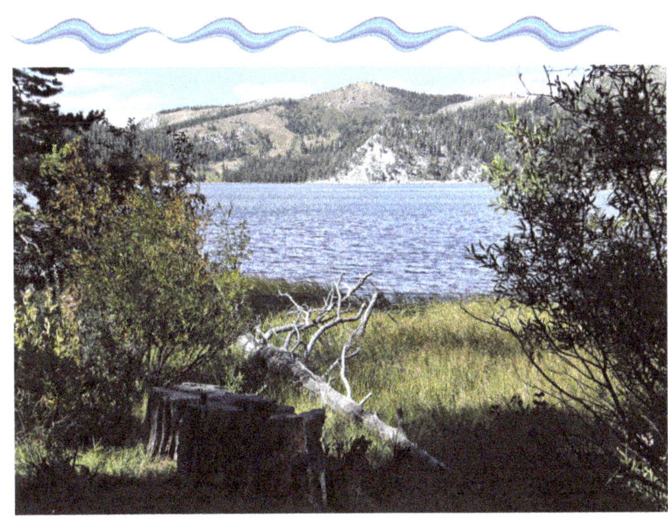

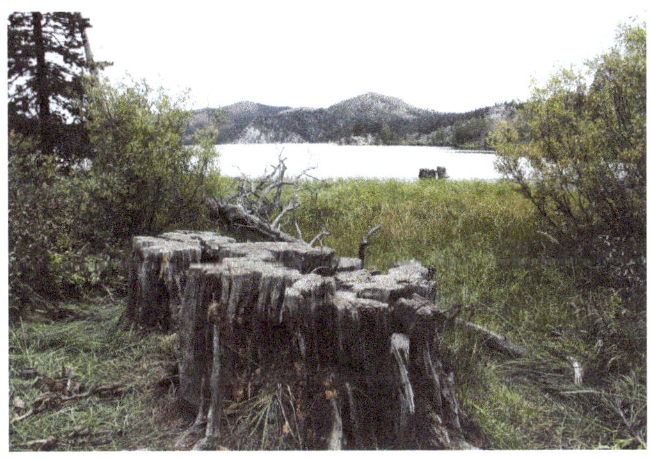

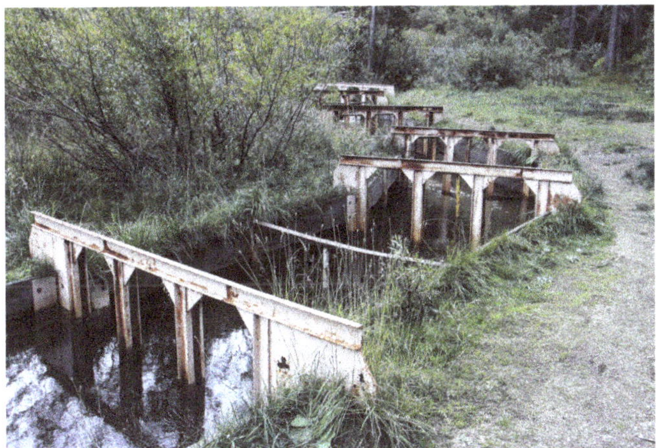

Marlette is the only state owned reservoir with Lahontan Cutthroat Trout living and breeding in it.

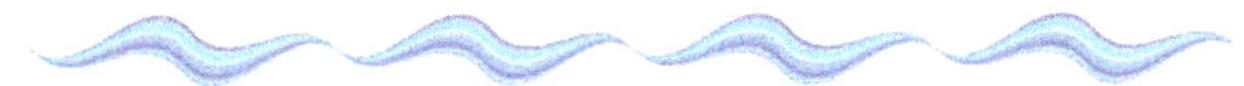

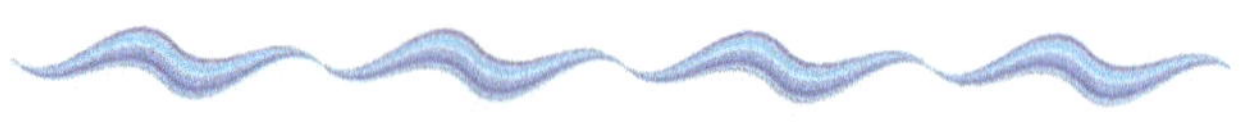

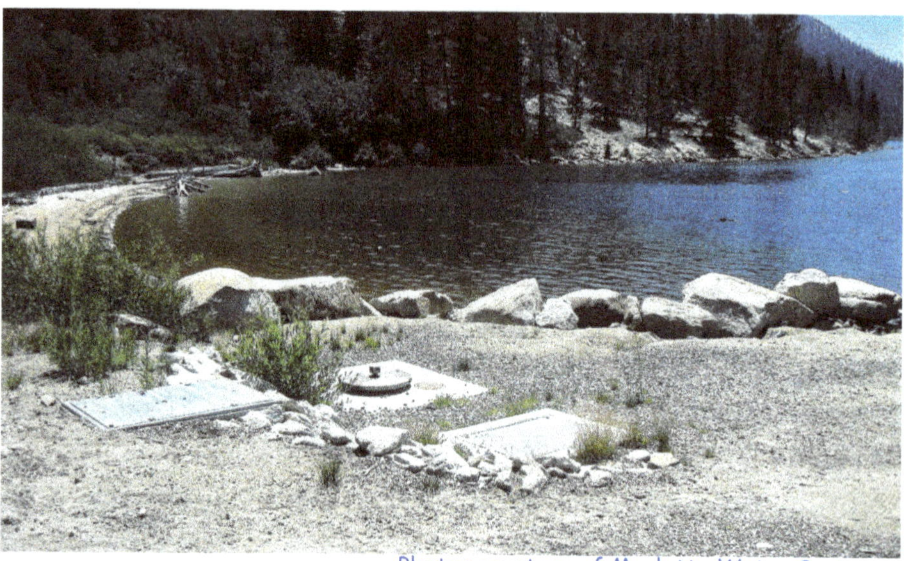

Marlette Lake
Pump Station

Photos courtesy of Marlette Water System

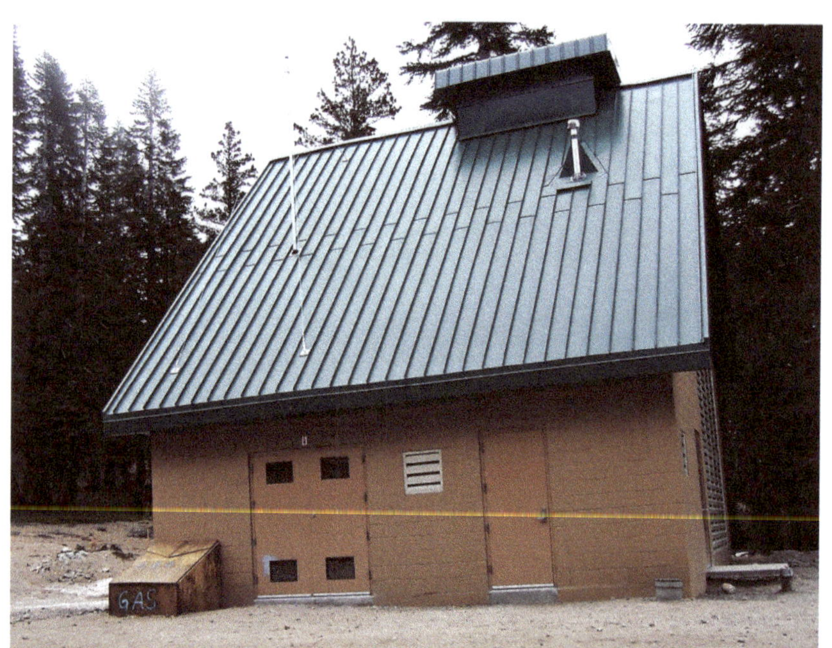

Marlette Lake Generator
Building which houses a
generator to provide power
to run the Marlette Lake
pumps.

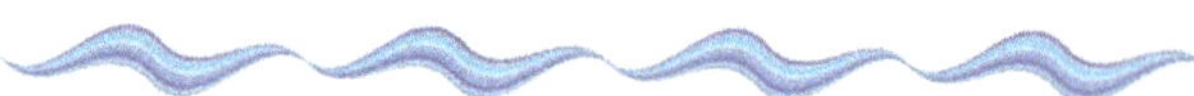

Photos courtesy of Marlette Water System

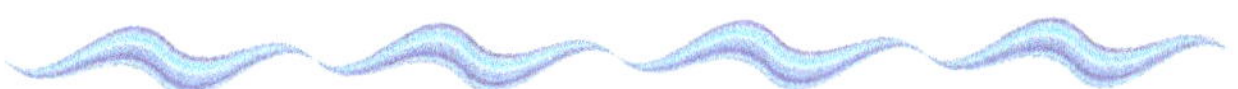

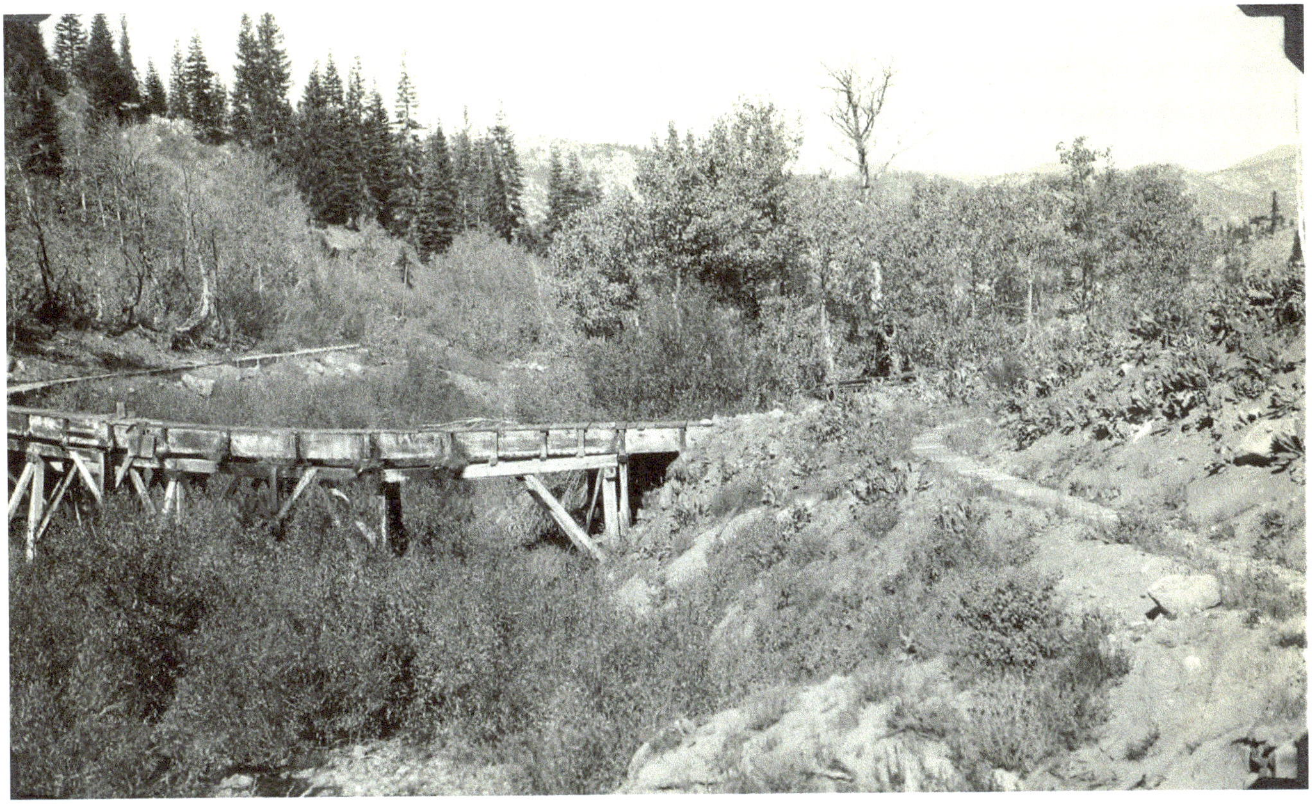

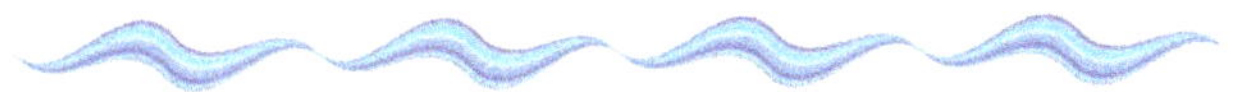

The original Flume below the
Red House Diversion Dam

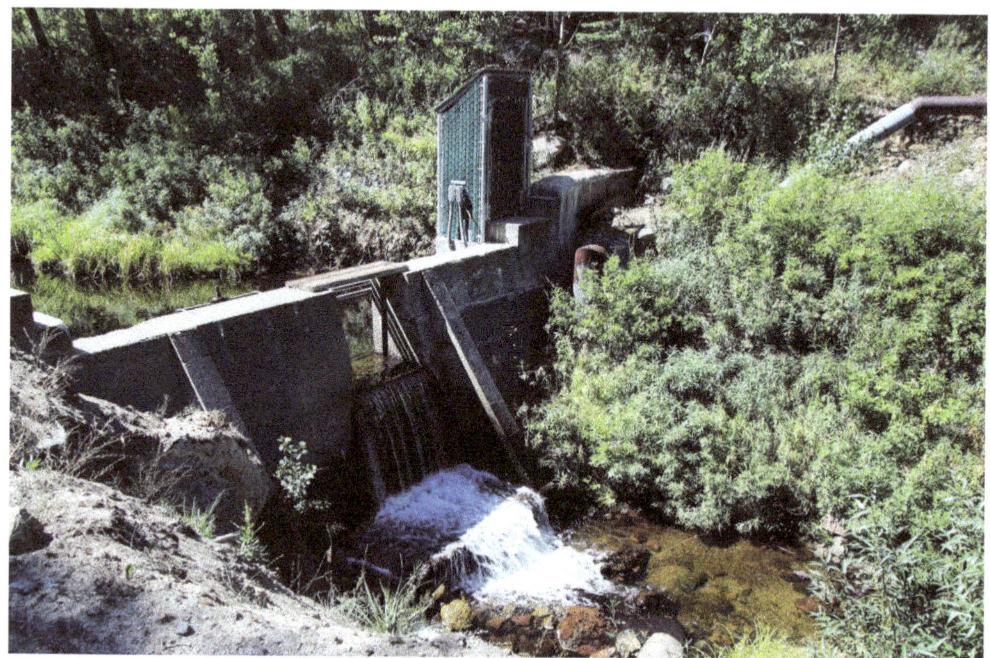

Red House
Diversion Dam

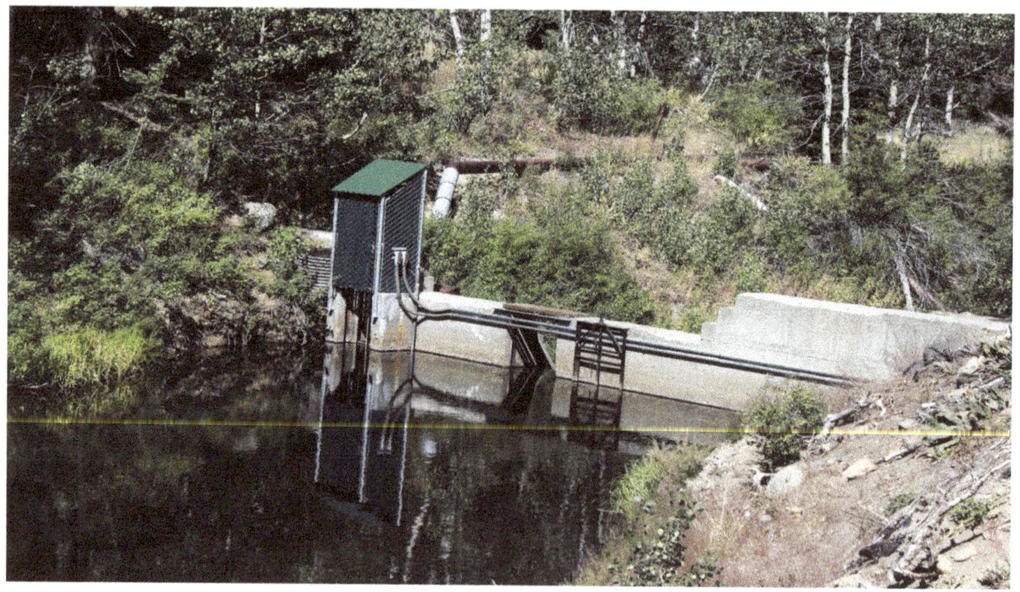

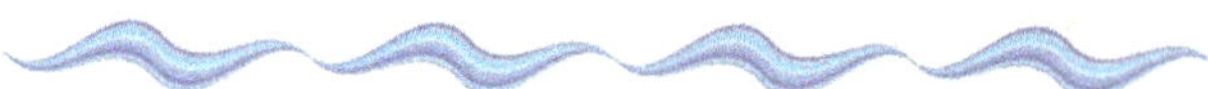

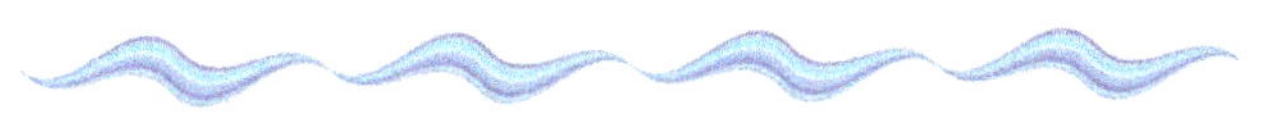

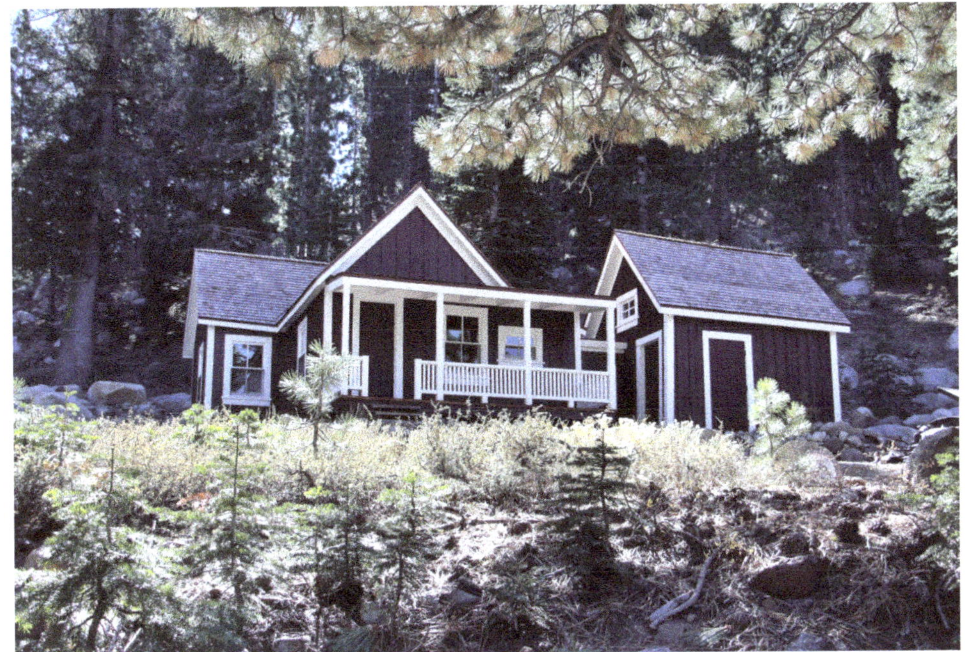

Red House
Diversion Dam
Tenders House
Built in 1877

Red House Water
Pipeline

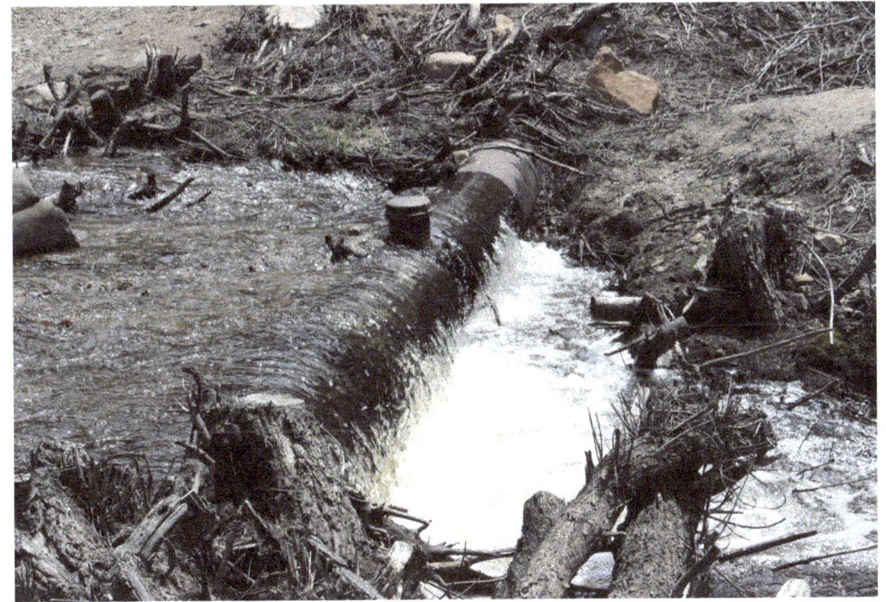

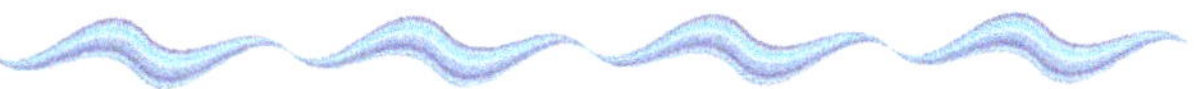

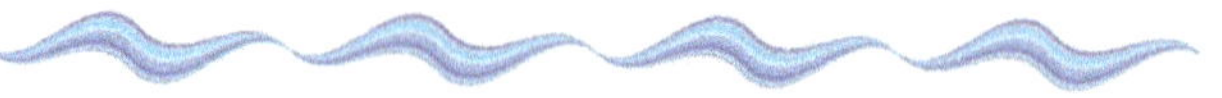

On the road from Red House to the water catchments

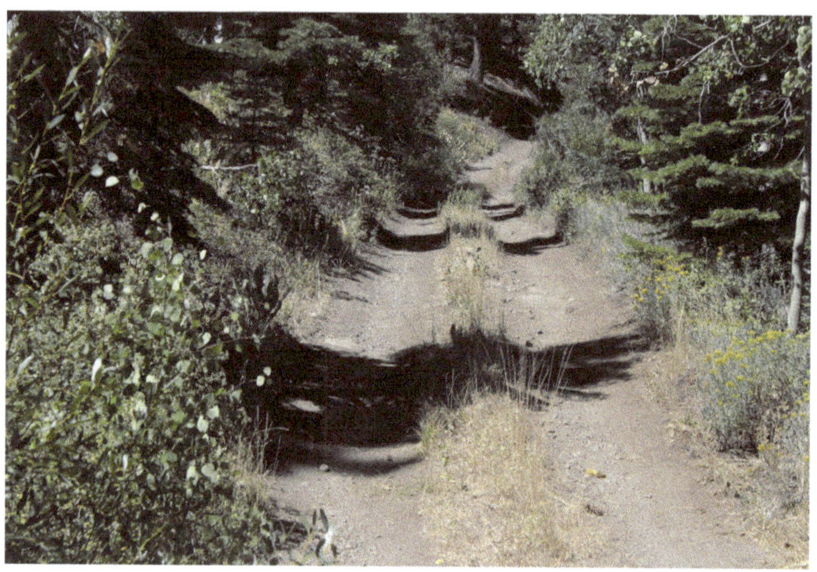

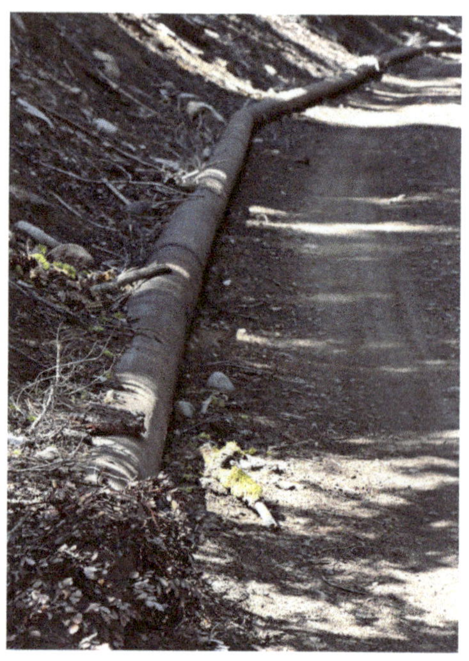

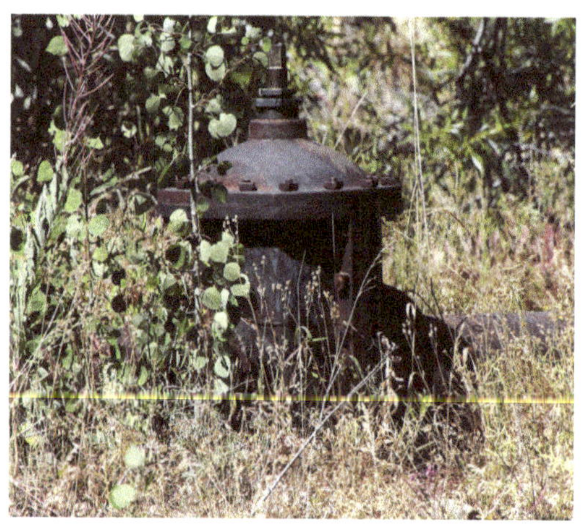

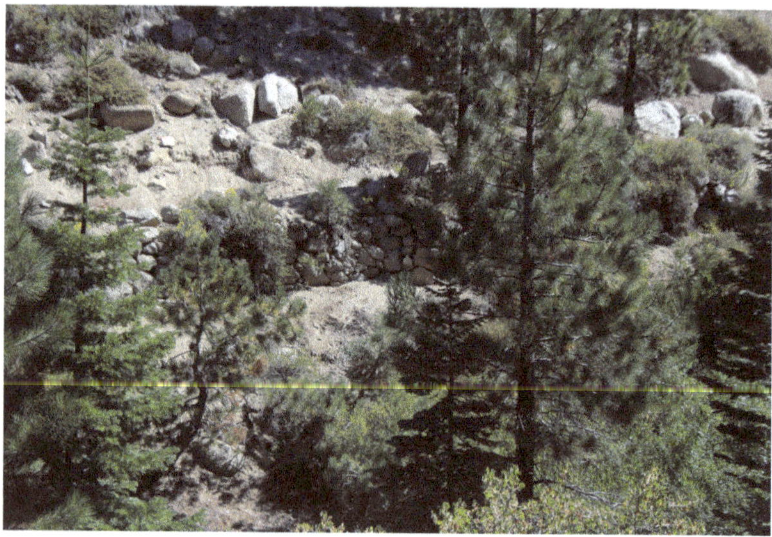

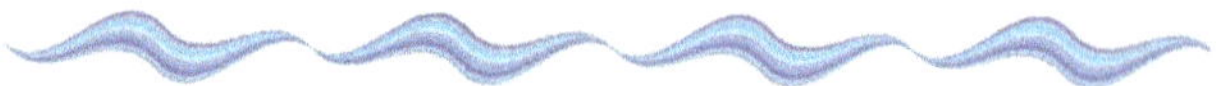

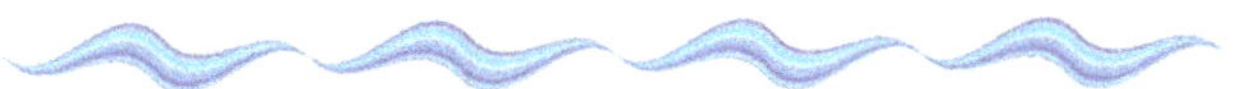

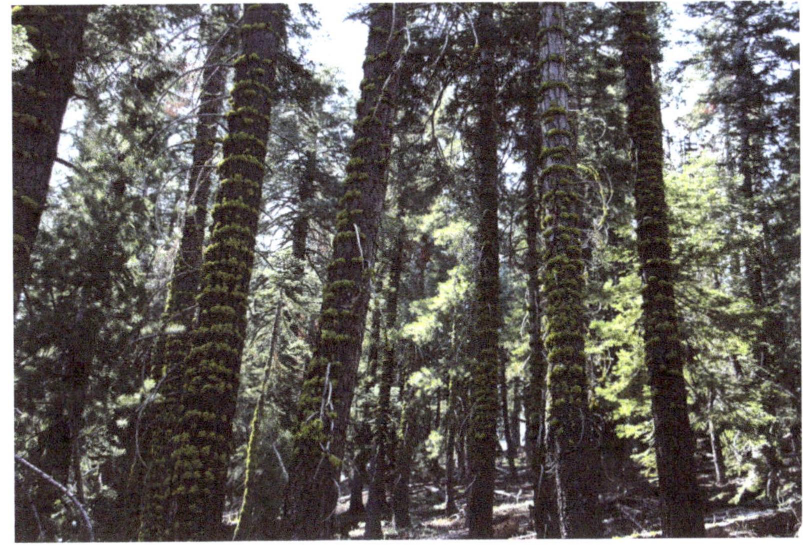

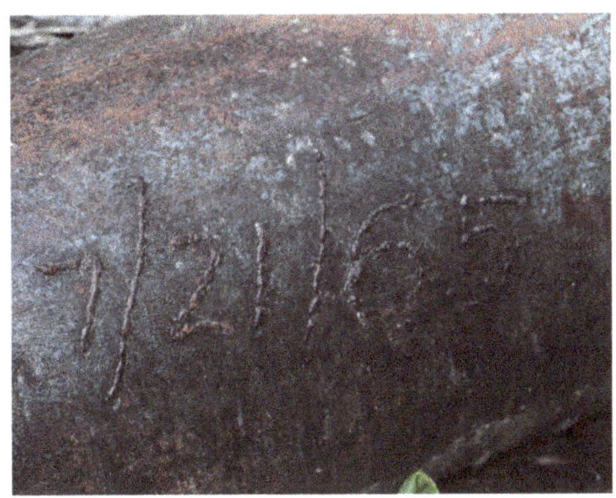

Original Pipeline

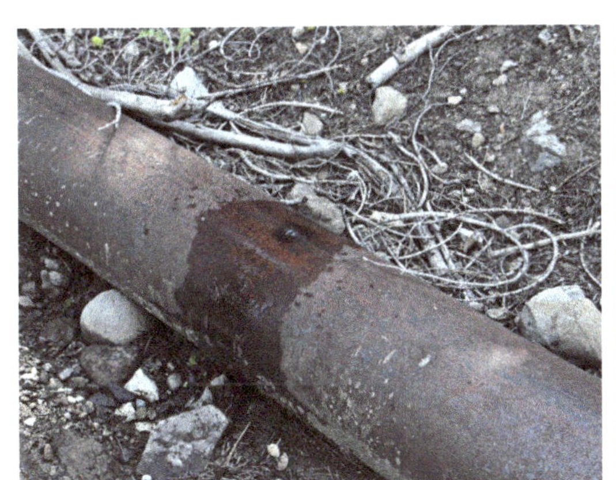

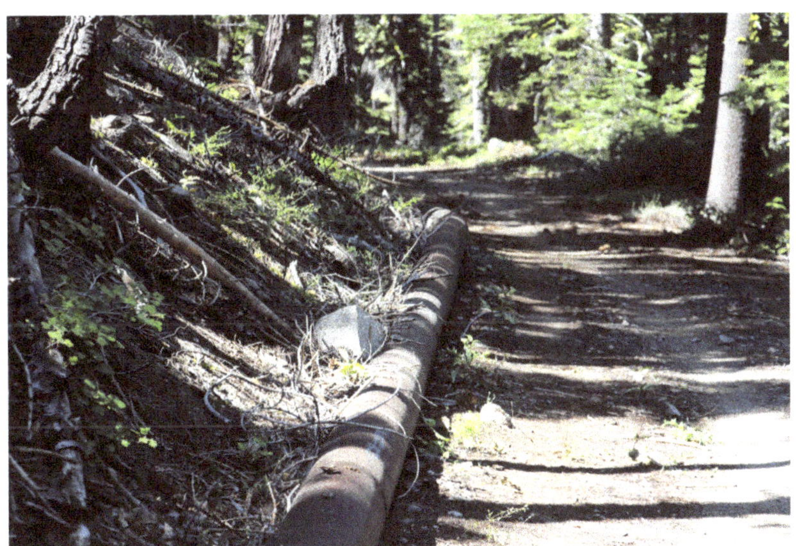

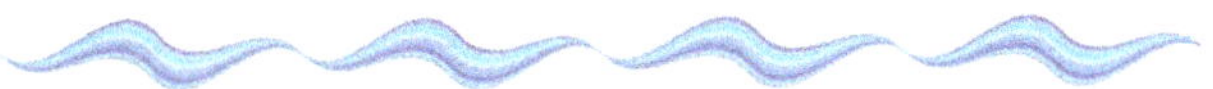

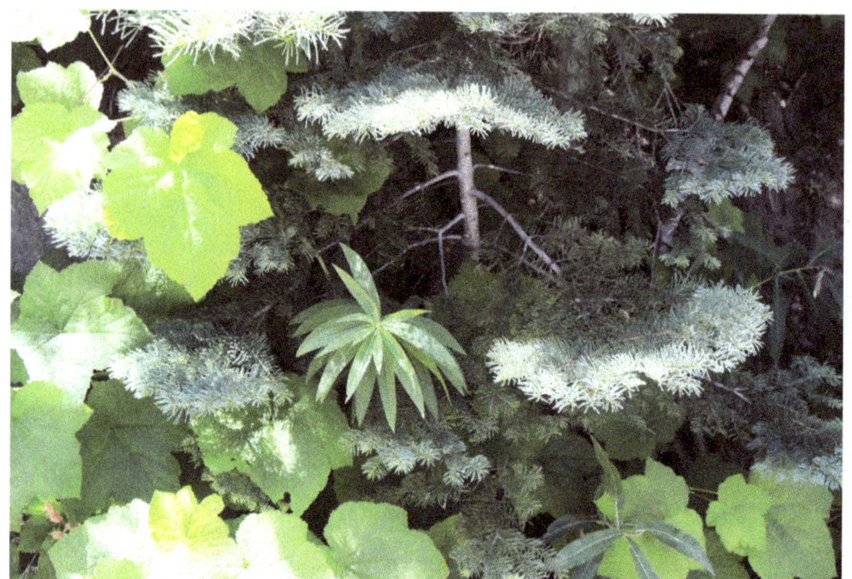

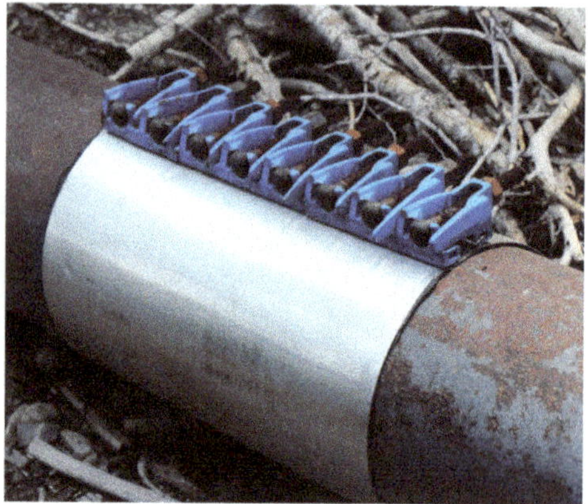

Pipe repair strap on
original pipe

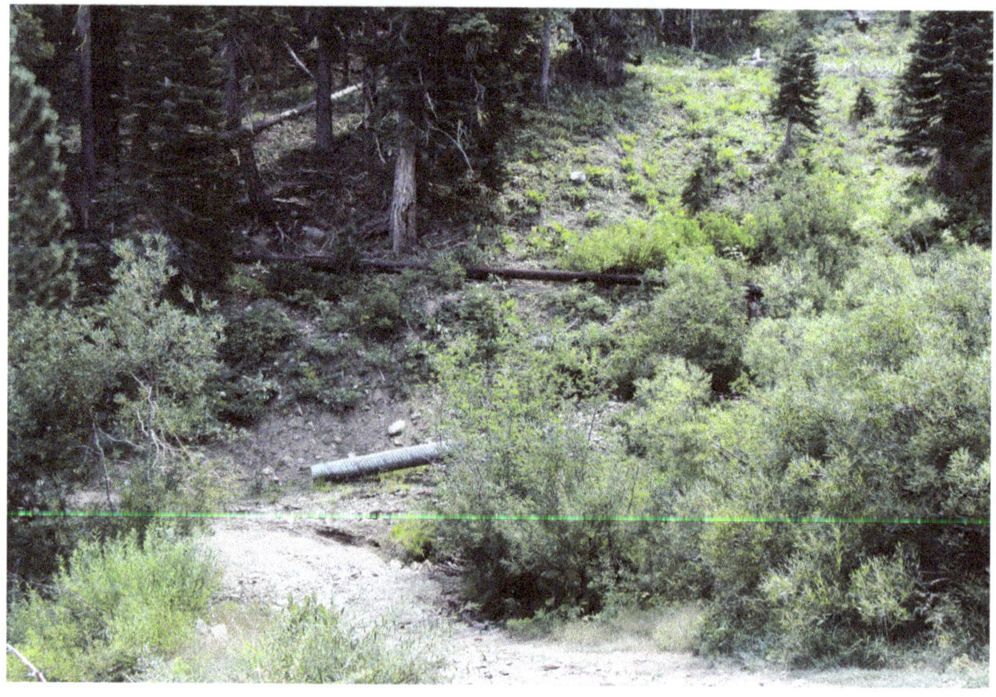

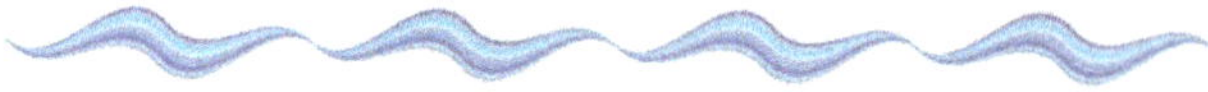

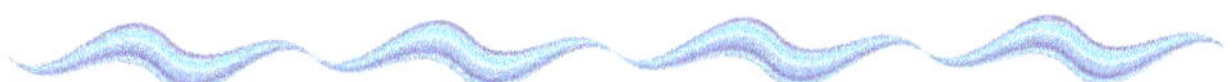

On the road to the water catchments

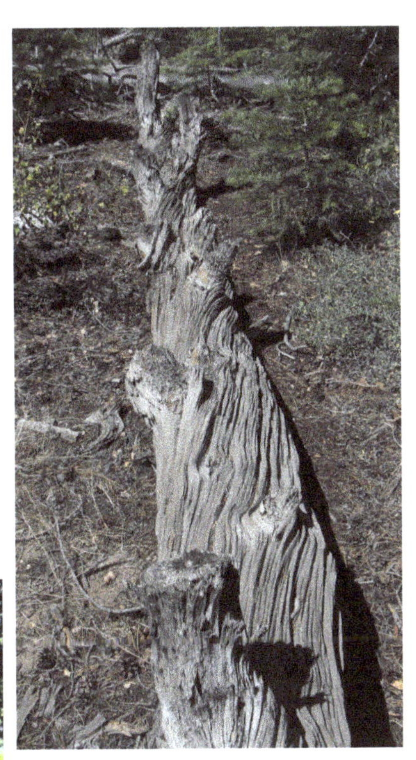

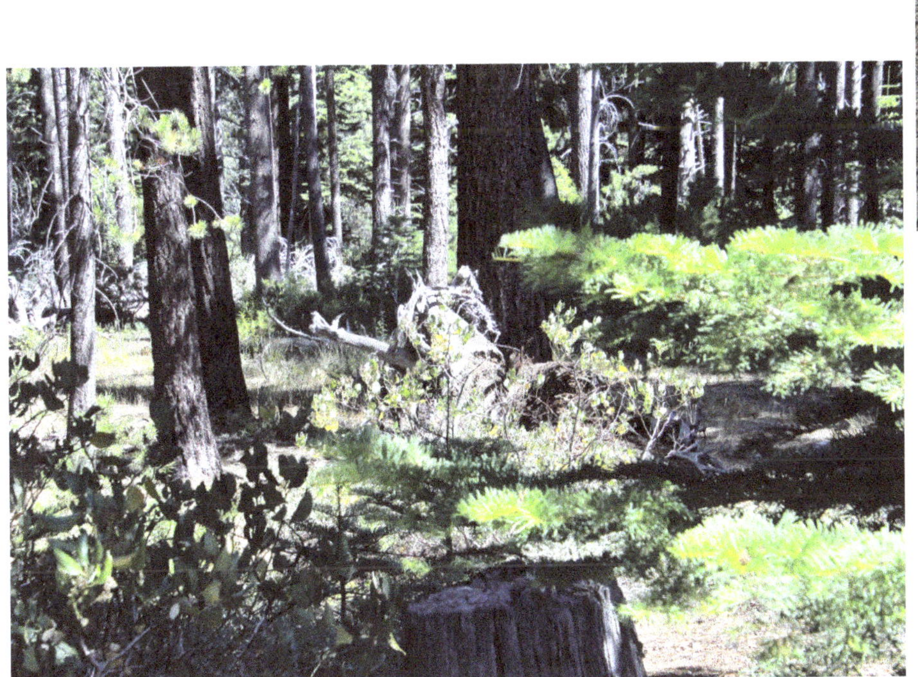

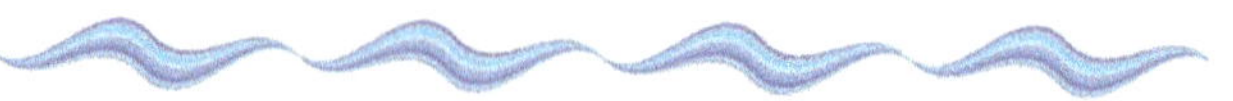

- East slop of the Sierras water catchments collect snow melt and run off water.
- They also collect water from the collapsed Incline Tunnel.
- The water directly feeds into the Red House Diversion Dam. There are six catchments.

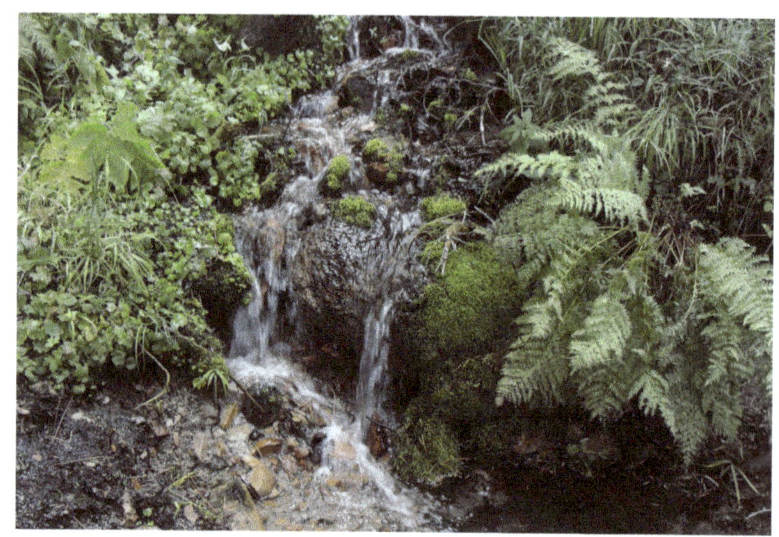

Catchment Number 6

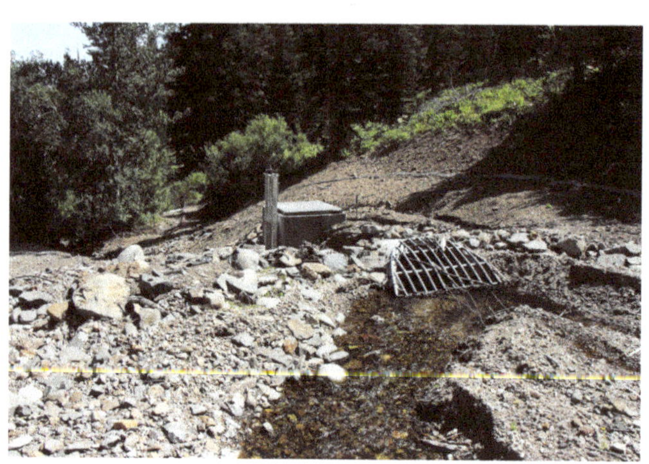

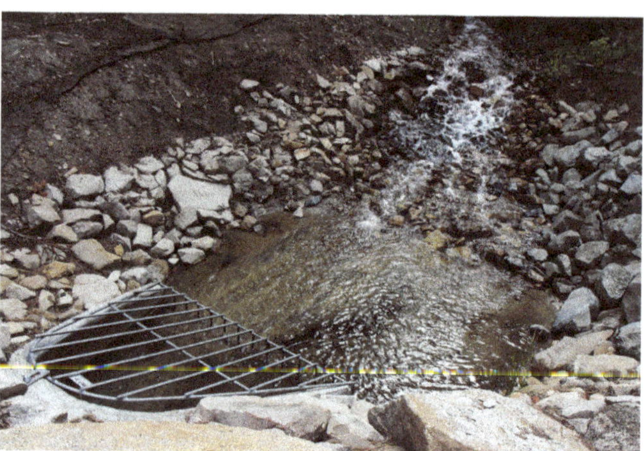

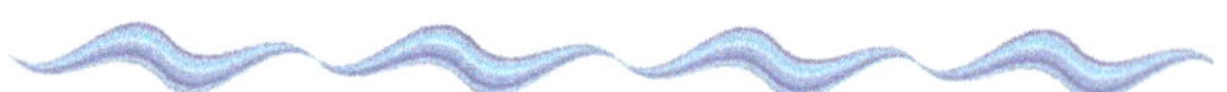

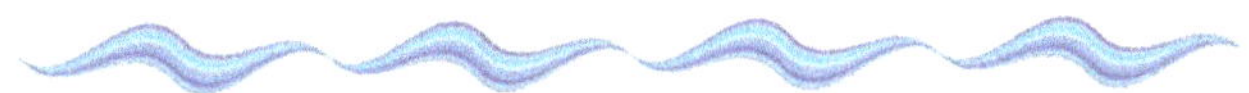

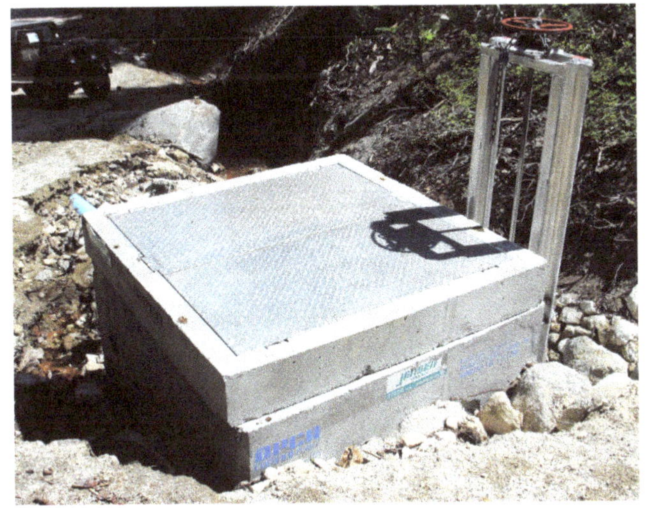

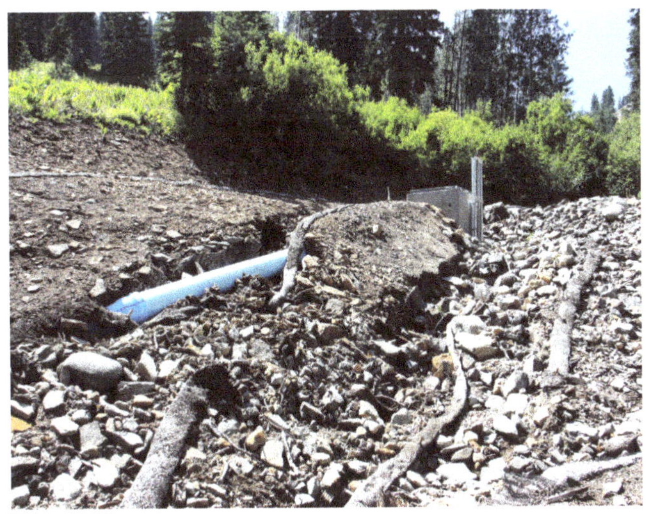

Catchment Number 5

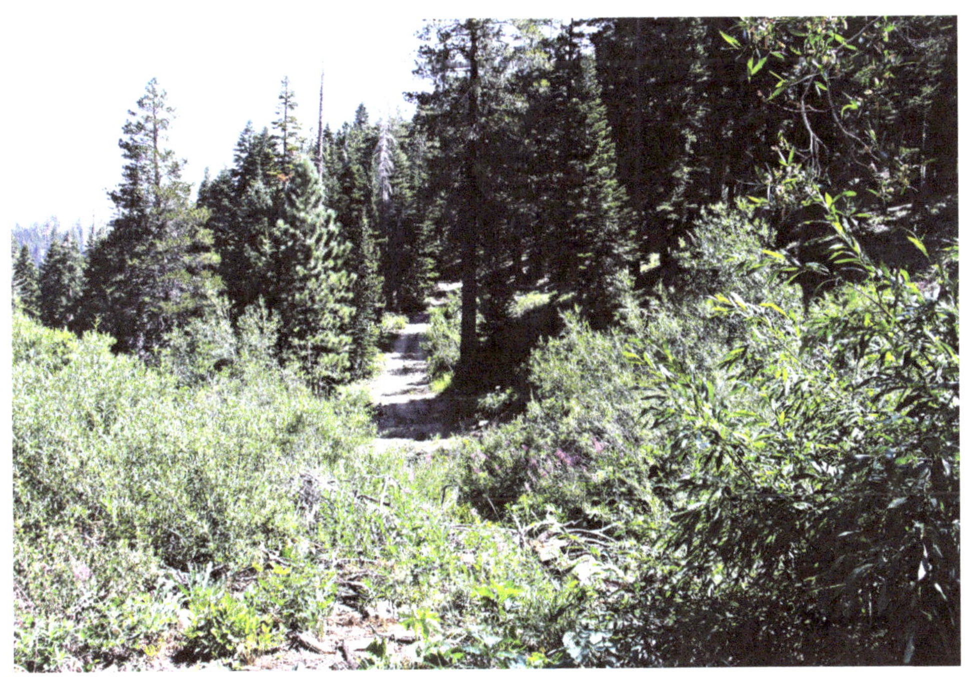

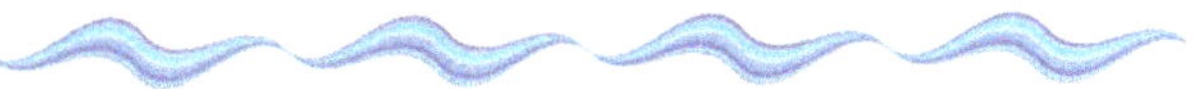

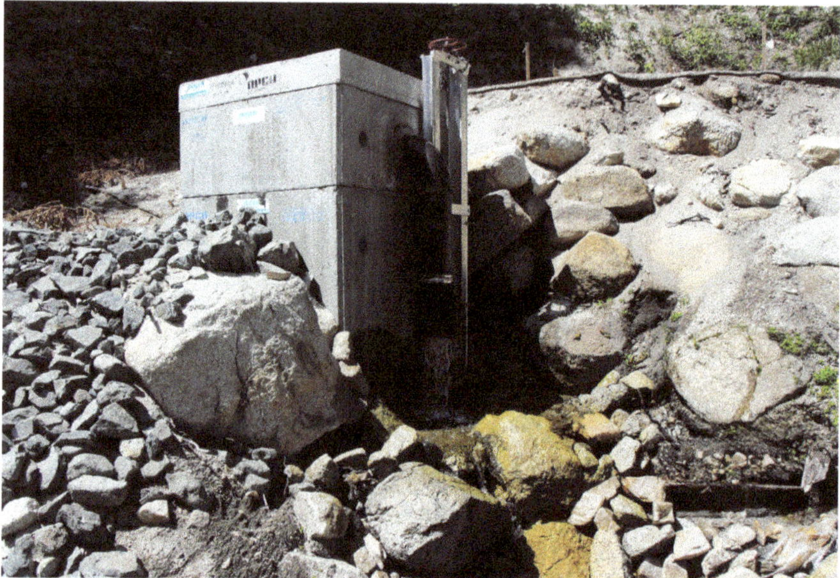

Catchment Number 4

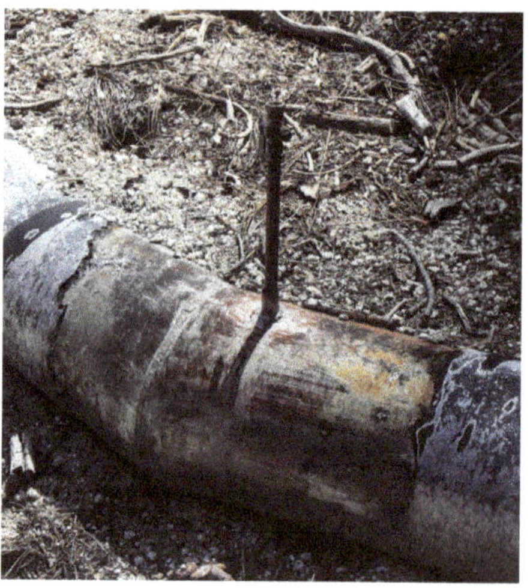

Air bleed in original pipe

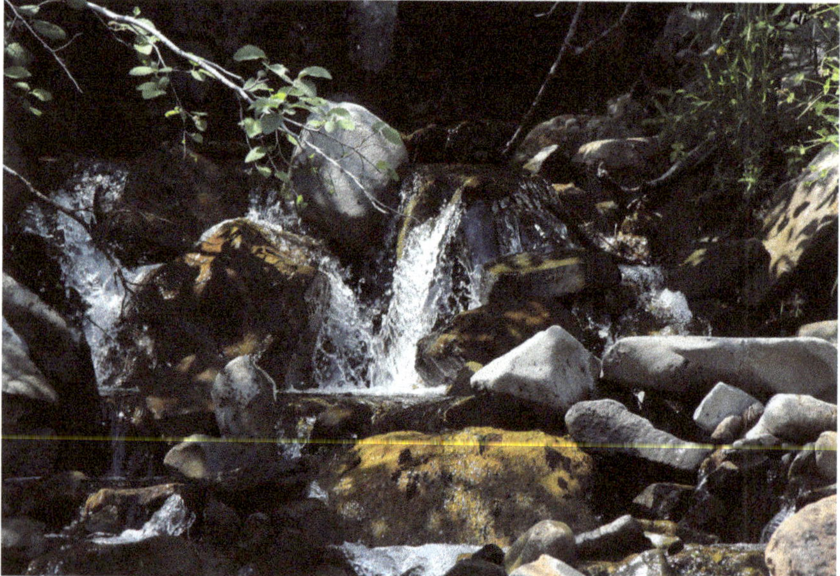

Little Valley

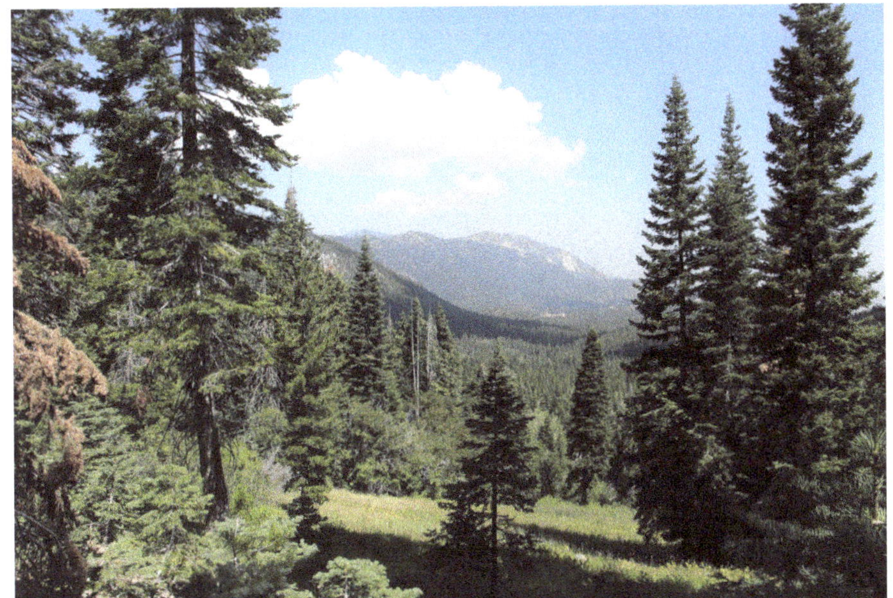

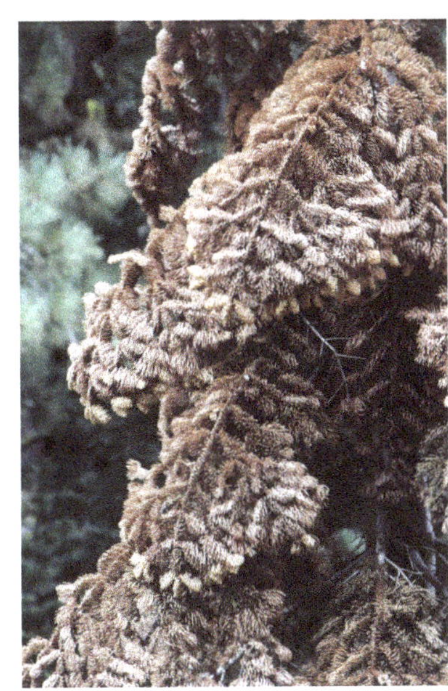

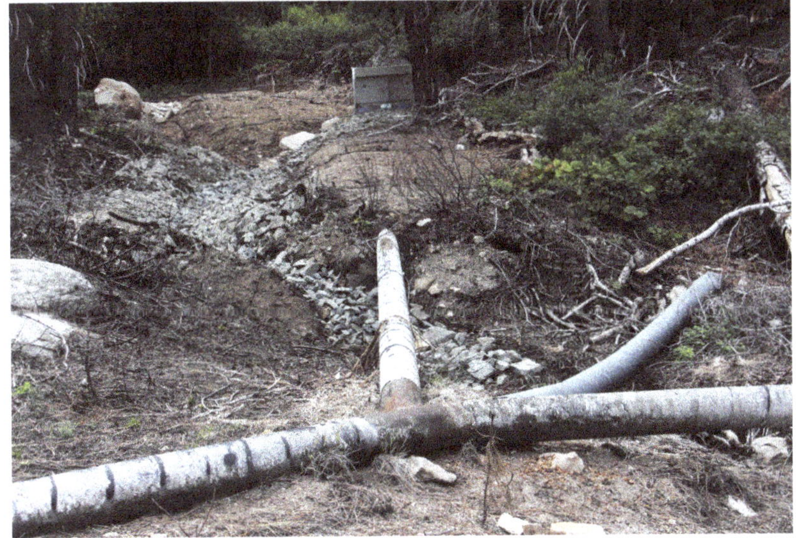

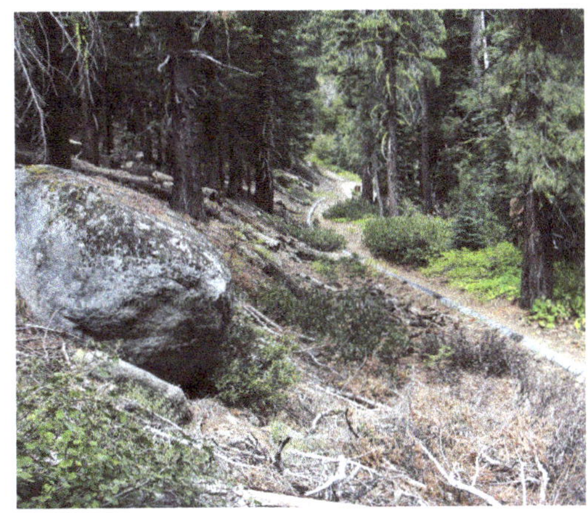

Catchment Number 3

On the swampy road to Catchment Number 2 and Number 1

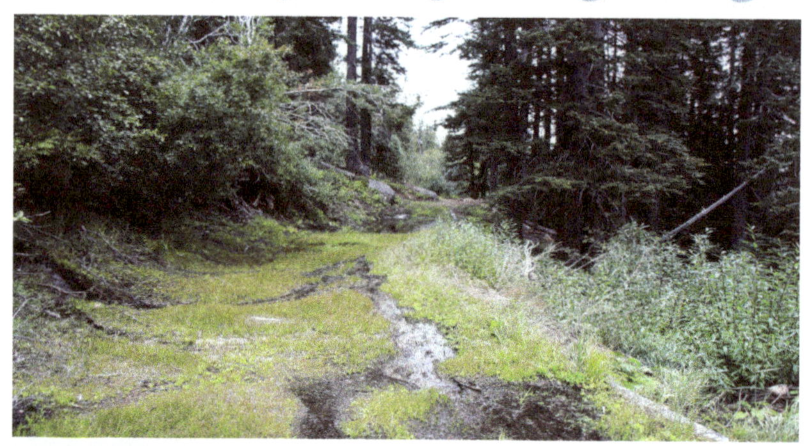

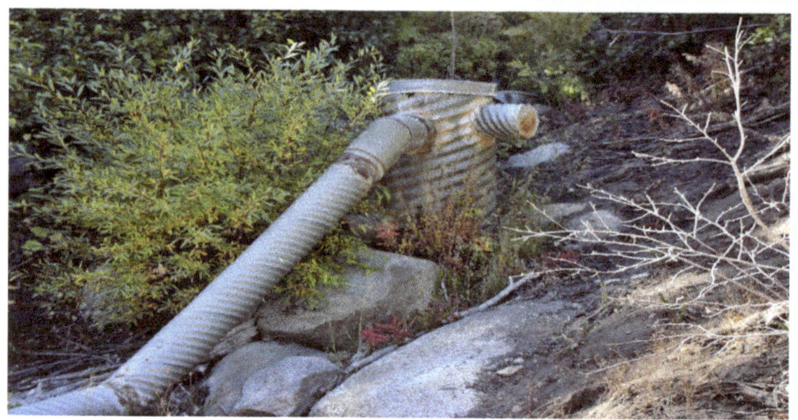

Catchment Number 2

Catchment Number 1

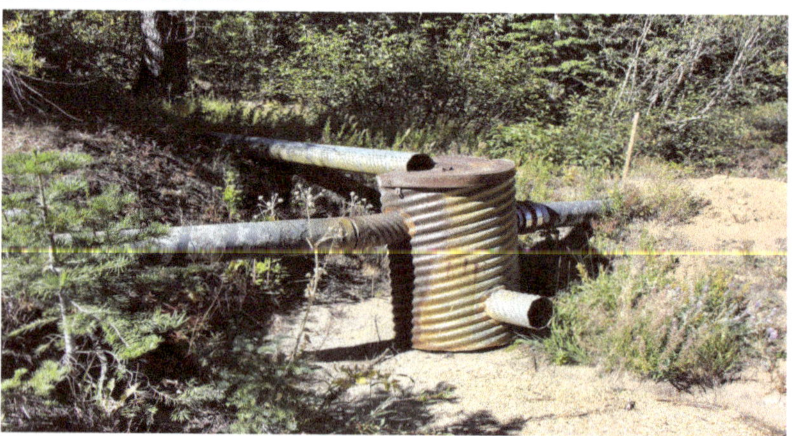

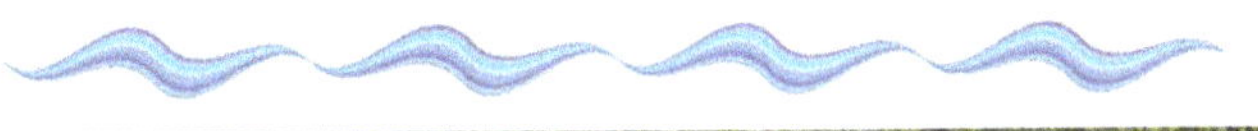

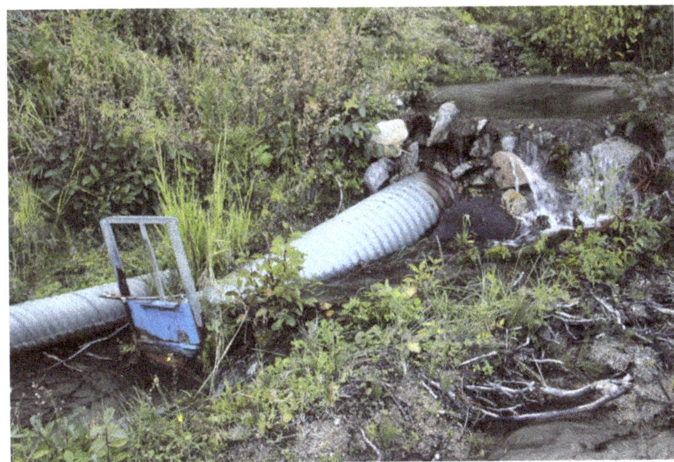

Catchment weir to capture the water flow from tunnel

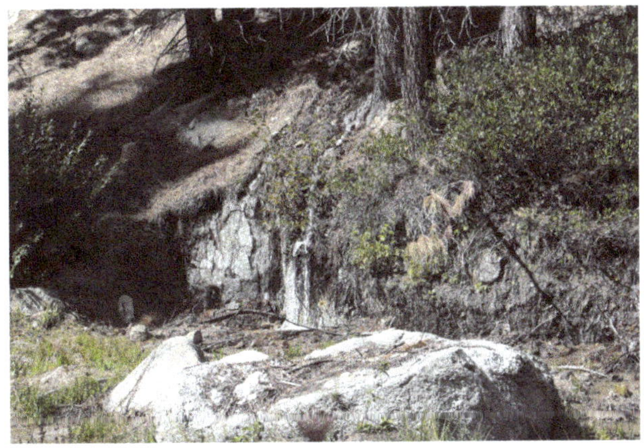

Incline Tunnel (East Portal) allowed water to go through the mountain from Marlette to reach the Comstock in August 2, 1877

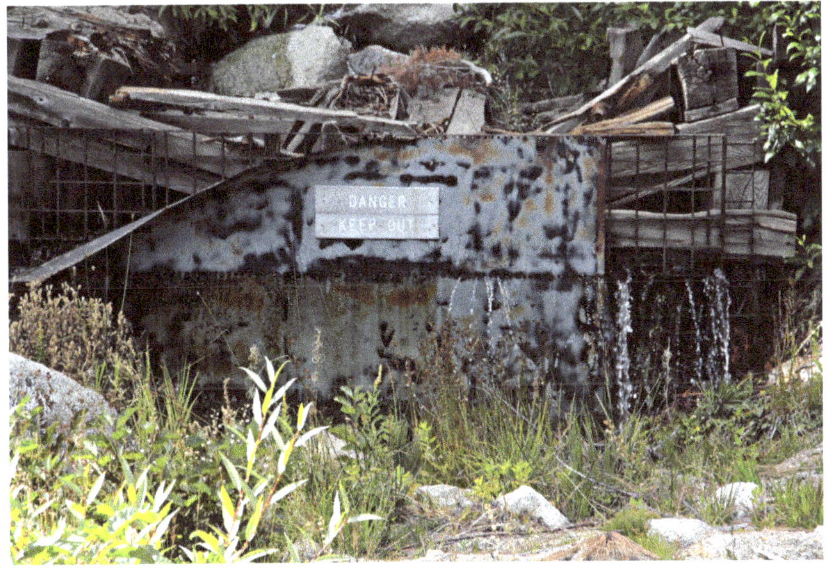

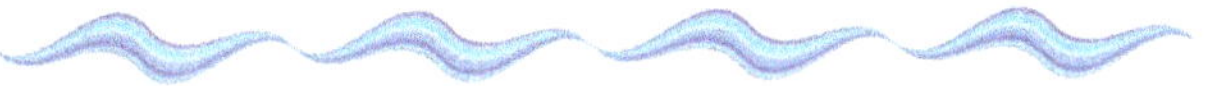

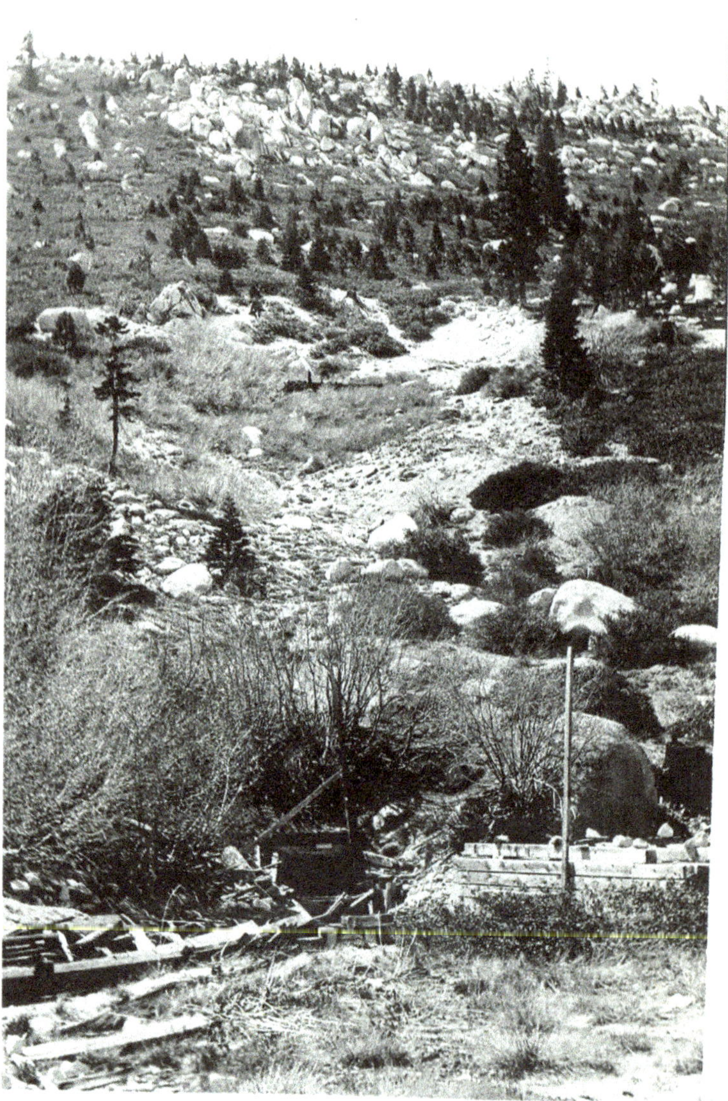

The east portal of the
Incline Tunnel which had
collapsed Circa 1957.

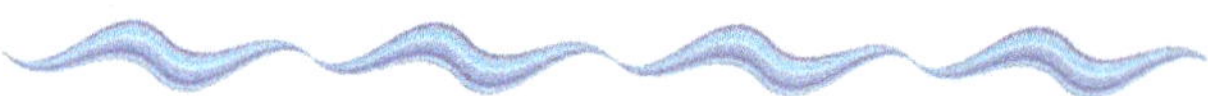

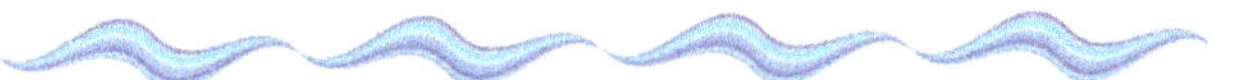

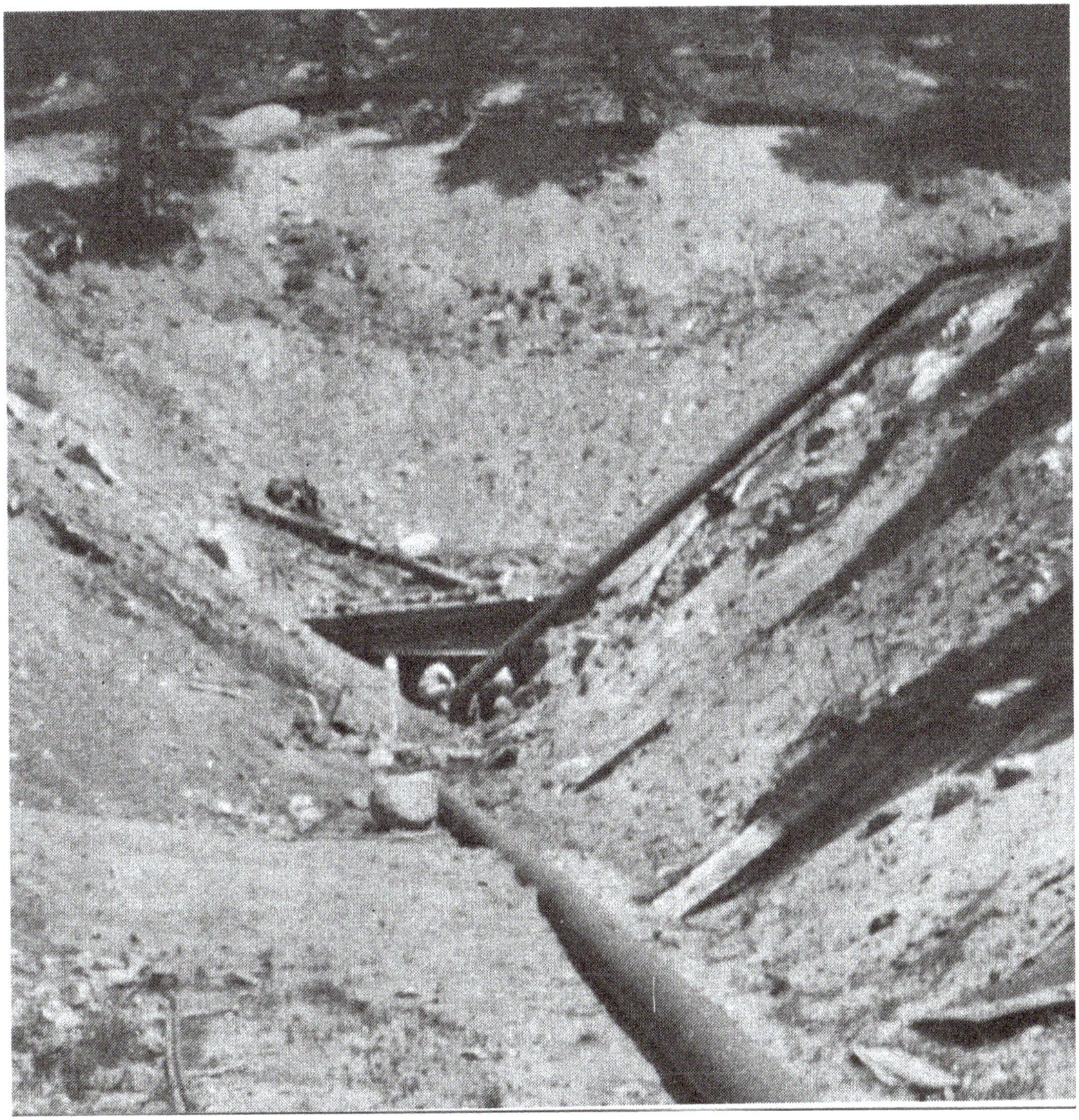

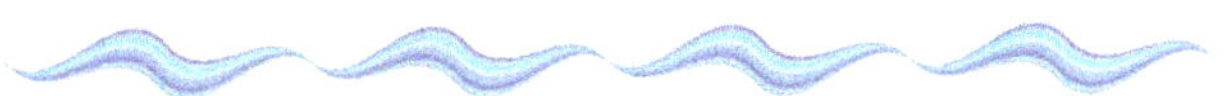

West portal of the Incline Tunnel allows
water to go through to catchment number 1

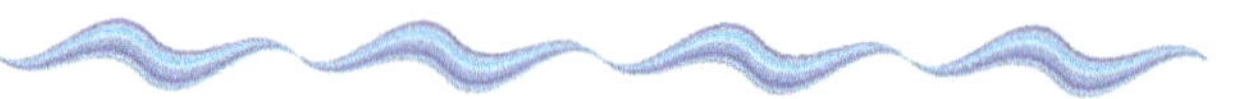

Lower Twin Lake

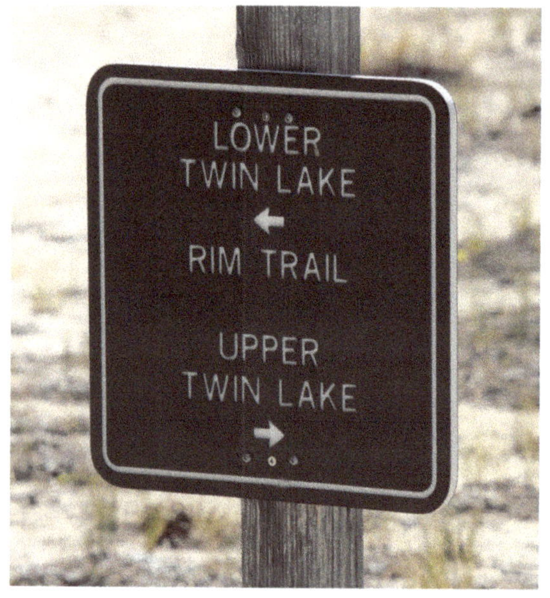

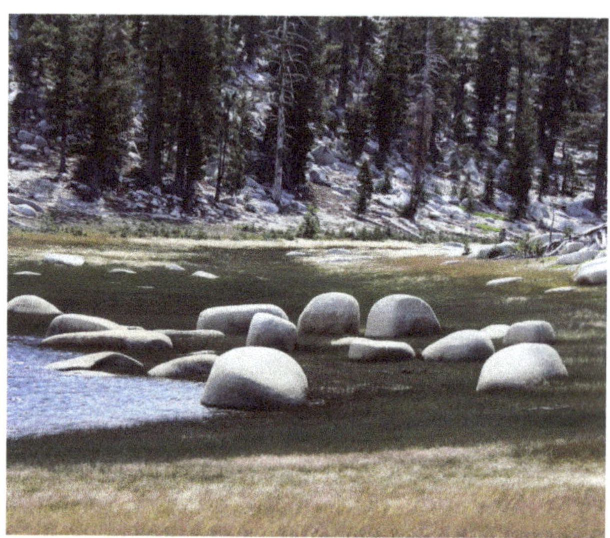

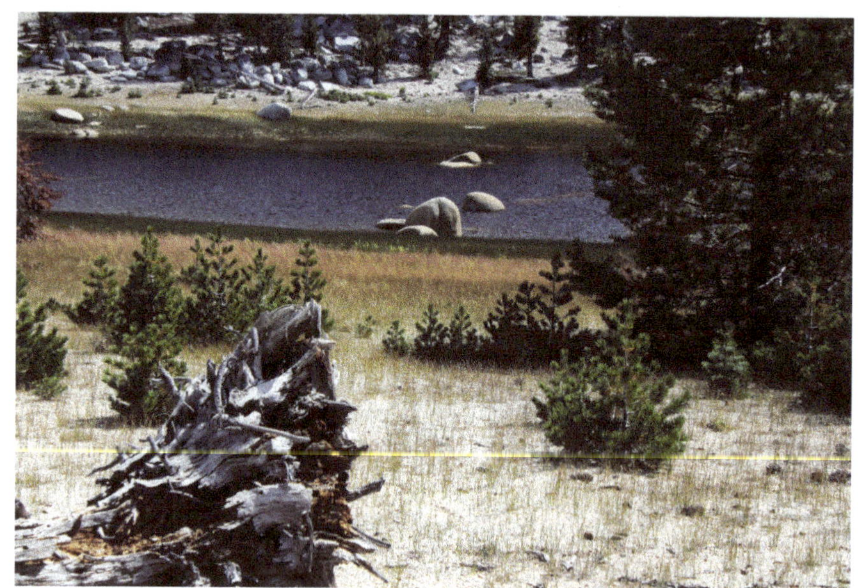

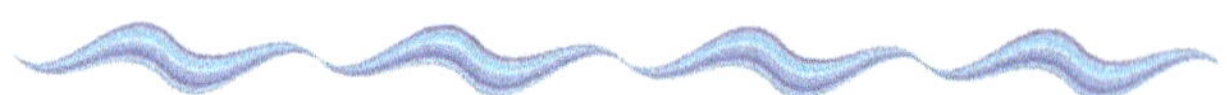

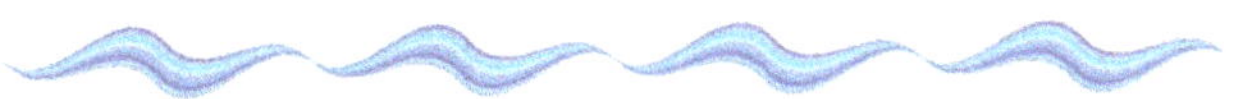

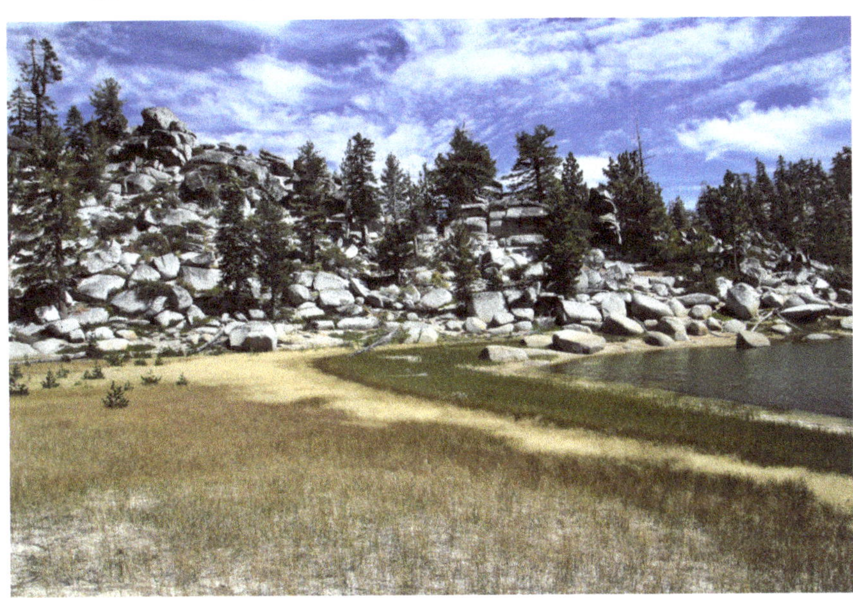

Upper Twin Lake

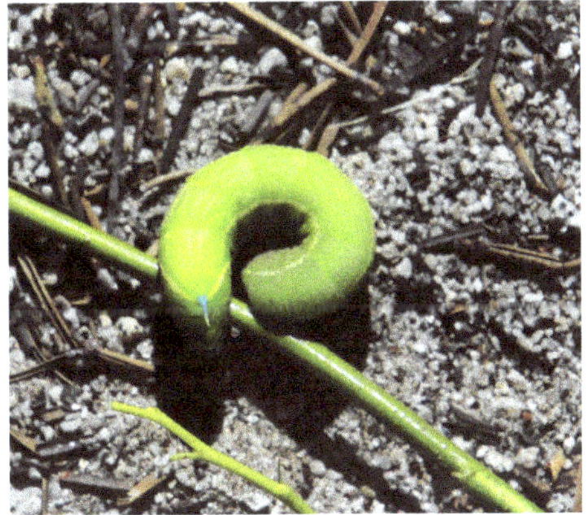

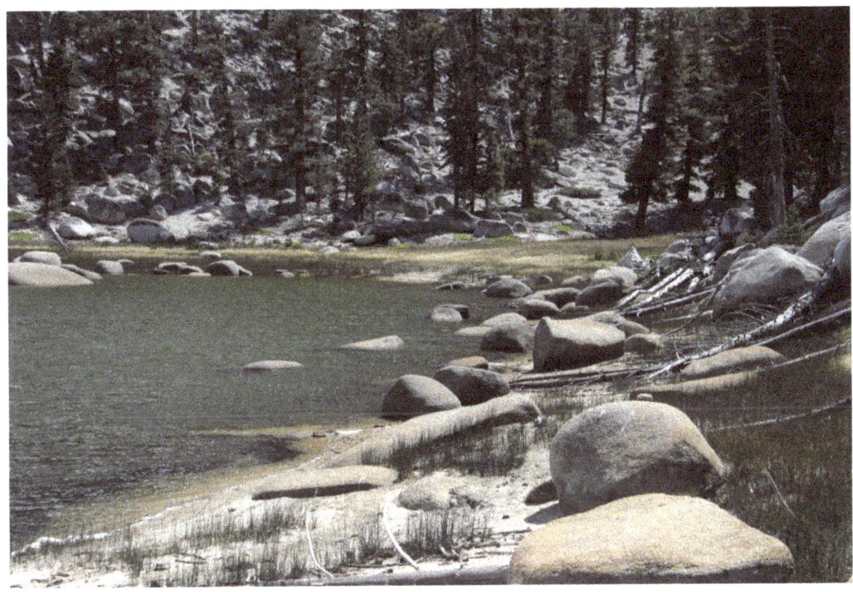

Pipeline Road to Lakeside Tanks

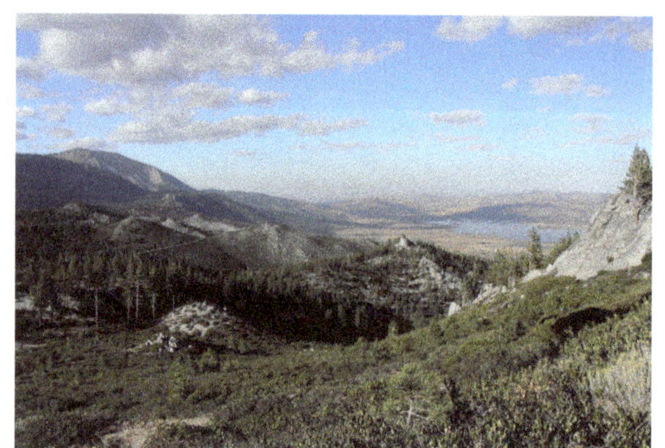

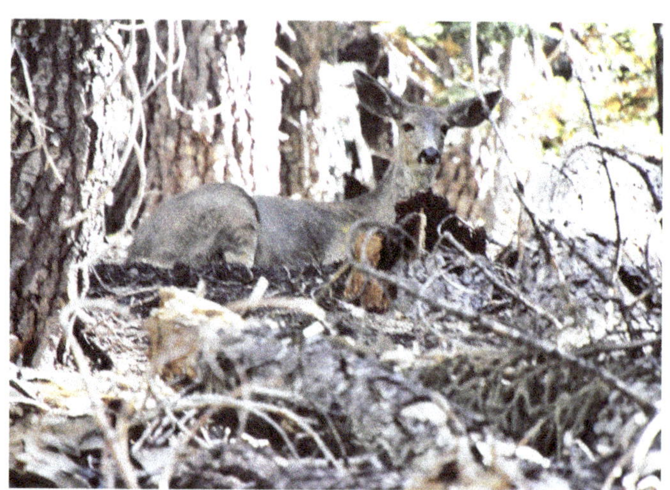

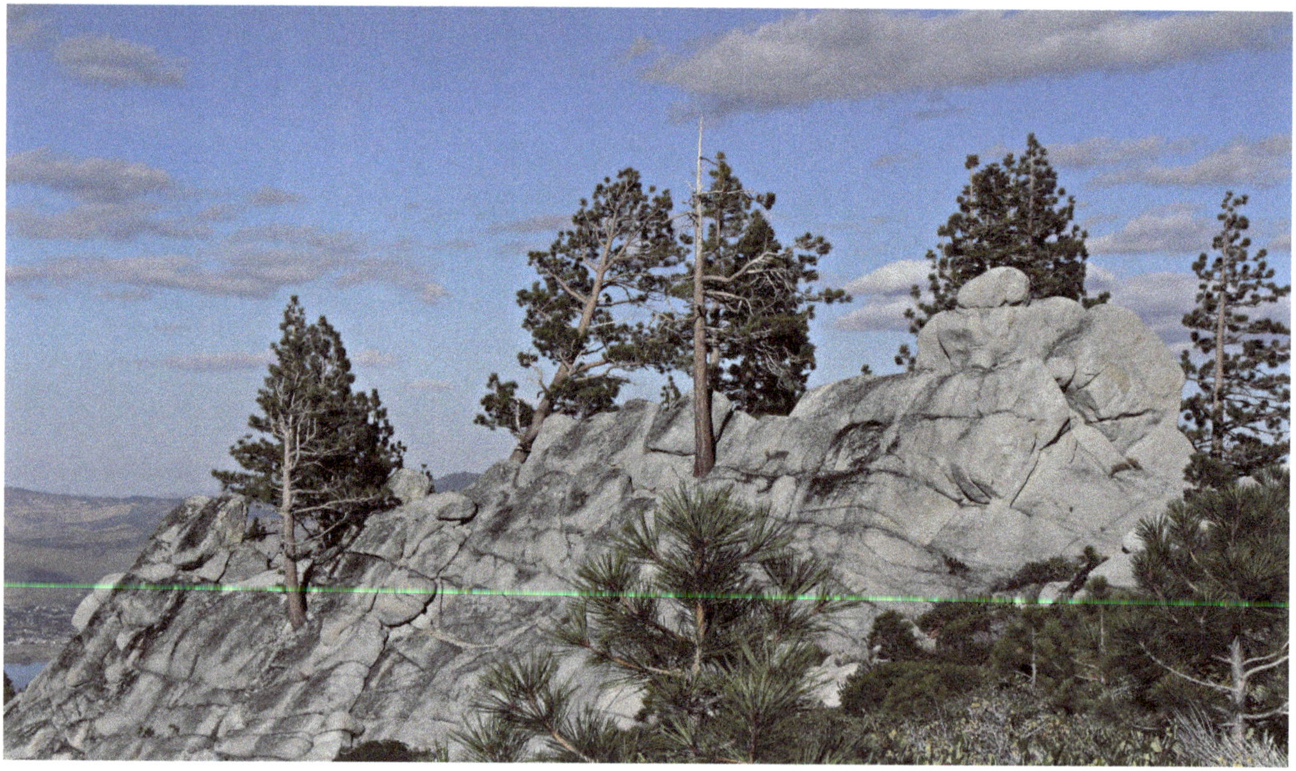

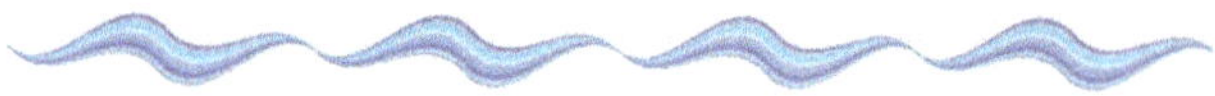

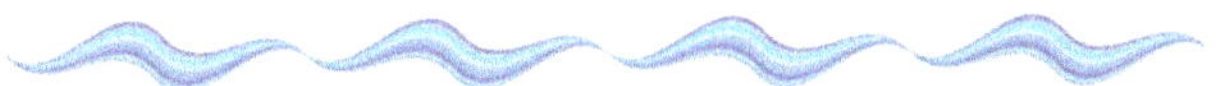

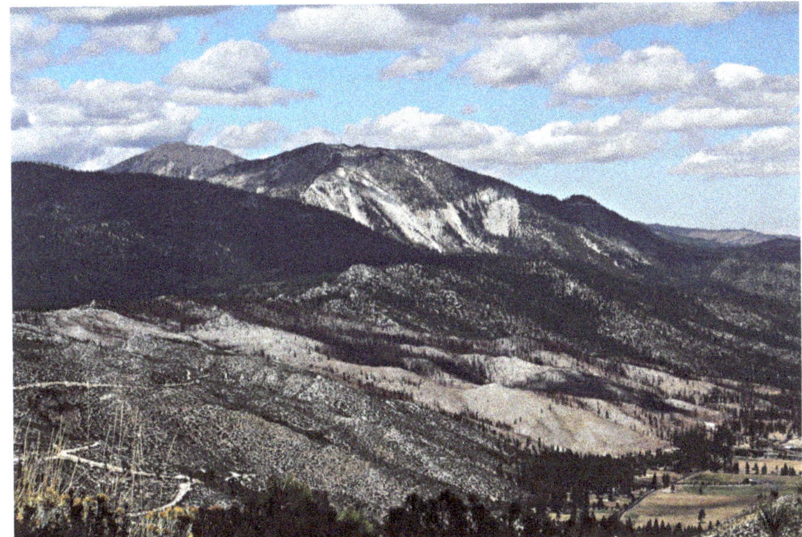

Slide Mountain from
Pipeline Road

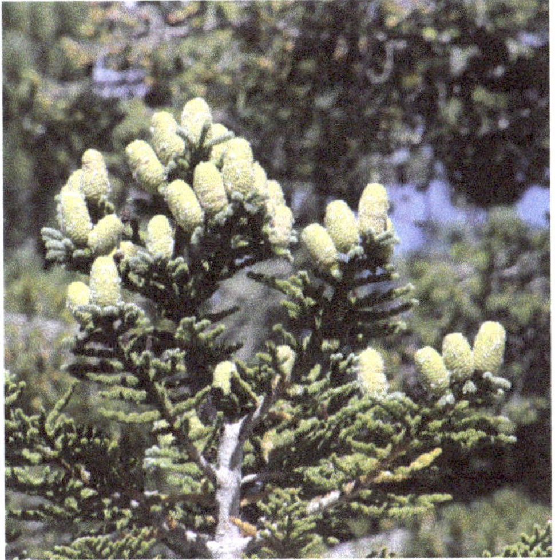

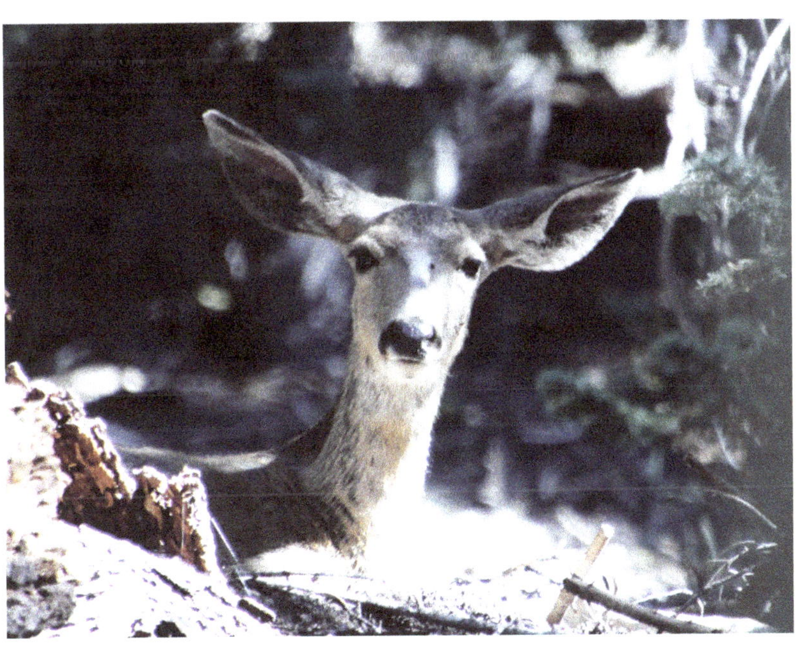

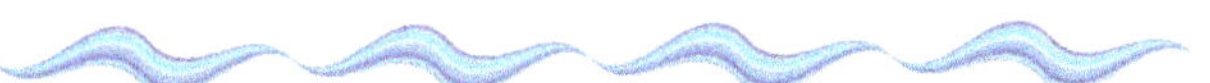

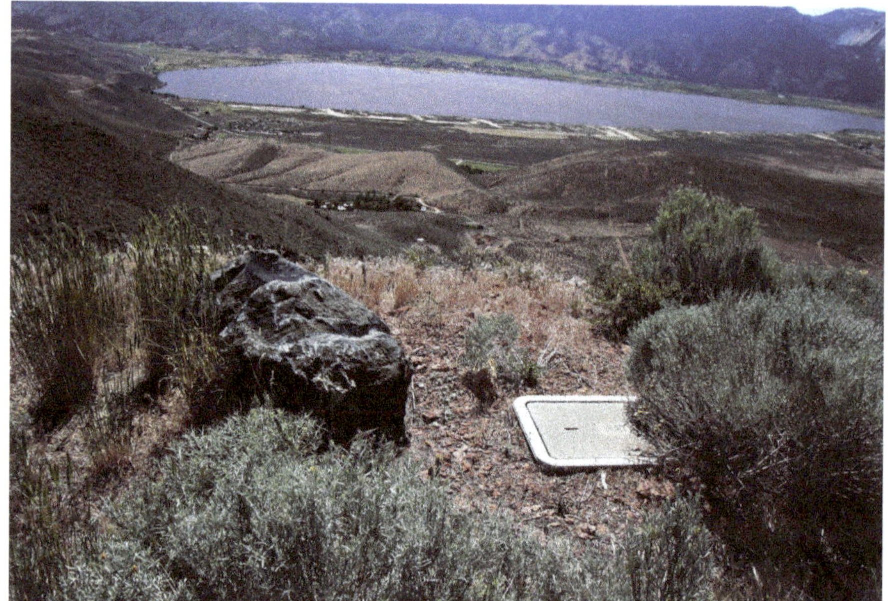

Water boxes along
Virginia City Pipeline Road
from Washoe Lake to
Five Mile Reservoir

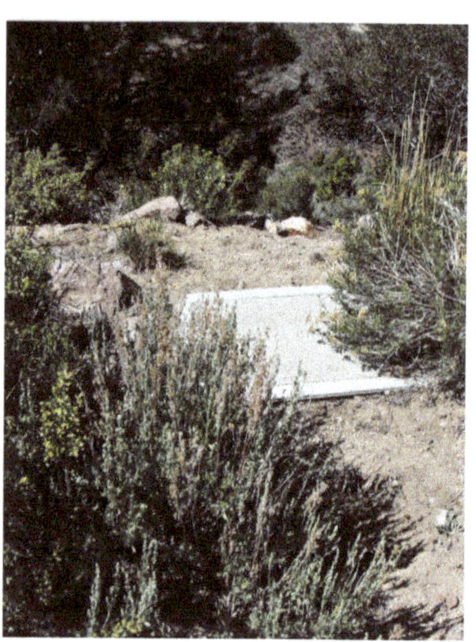

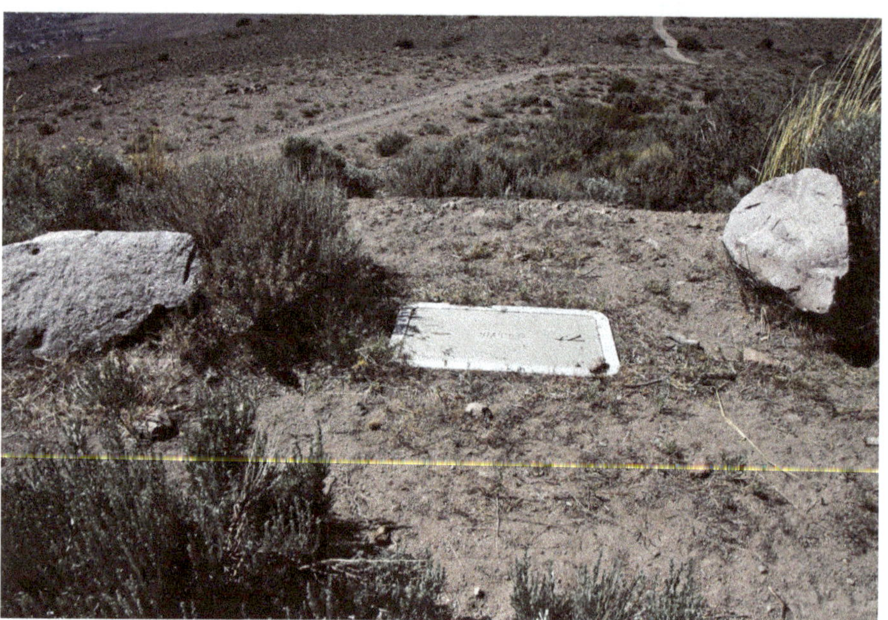

Washoe Lake from East Side Pipeline Road

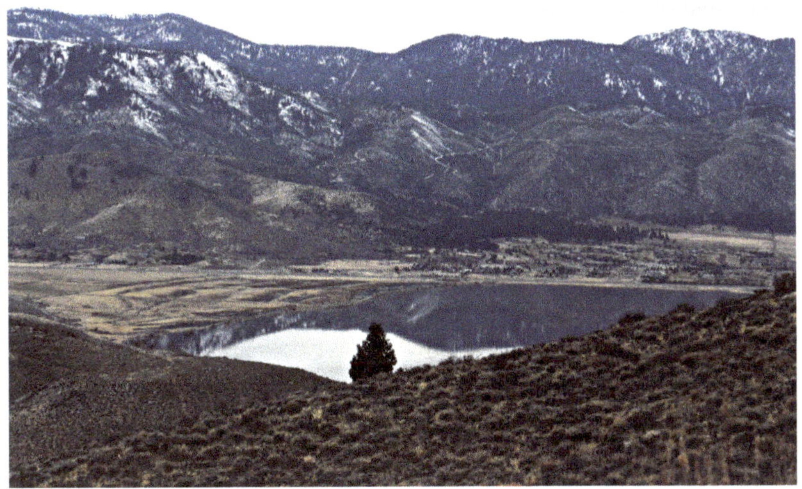

Flumes from Five Mile Reservoir
to Virginia City, C. 1877

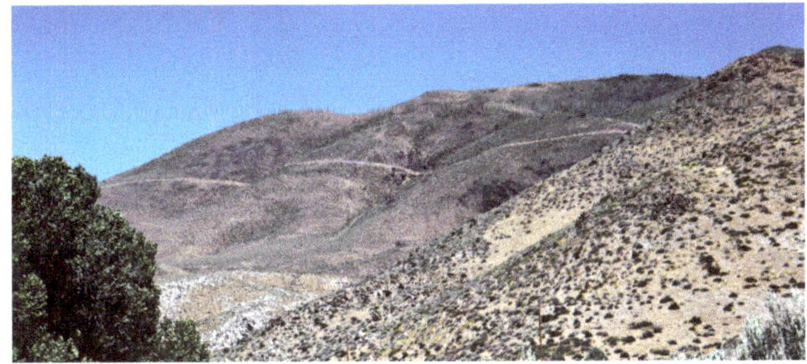

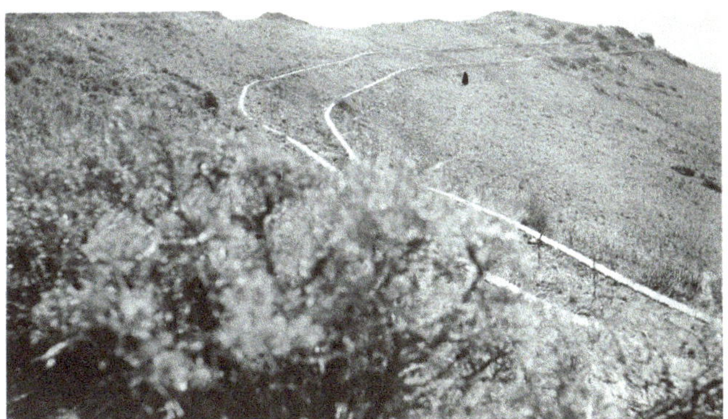

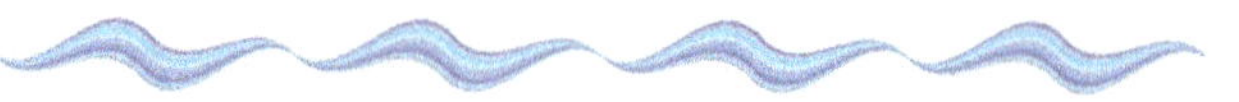

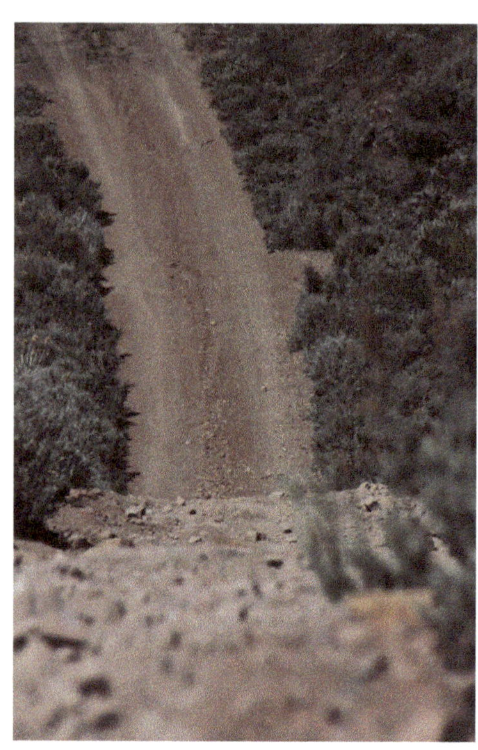

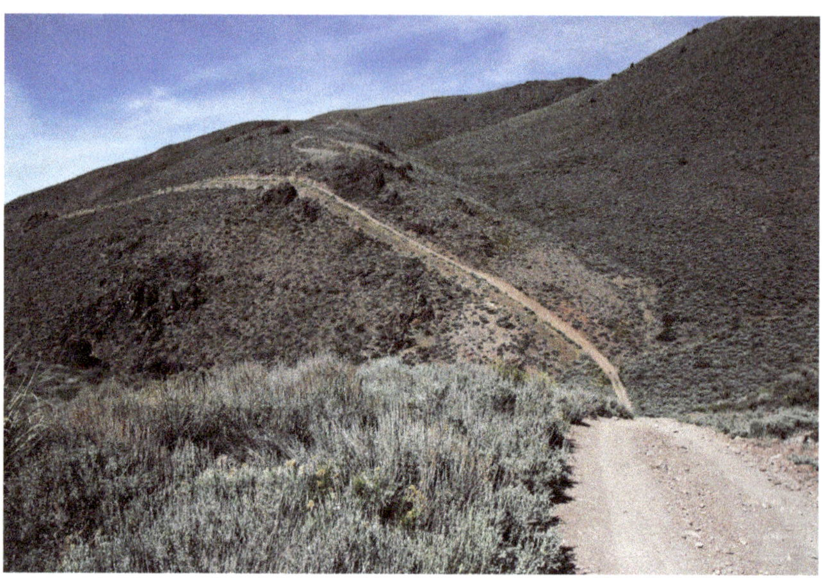

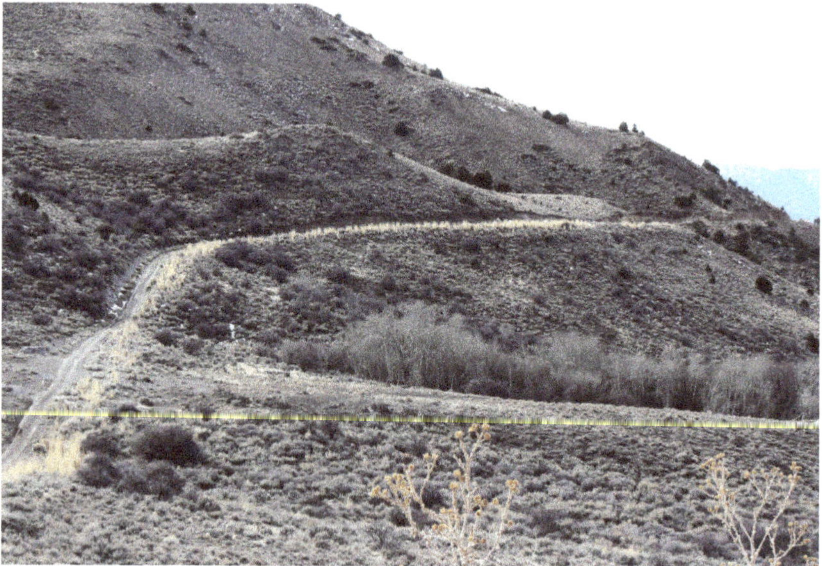

Virginia City Pipeline
Road from the Washoe
Lake to Five Mile
Reservoir

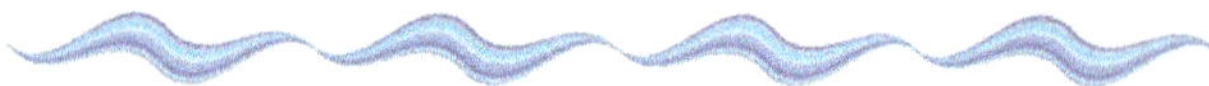

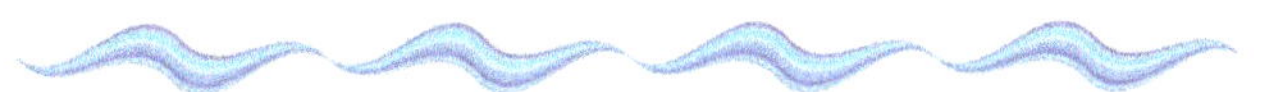

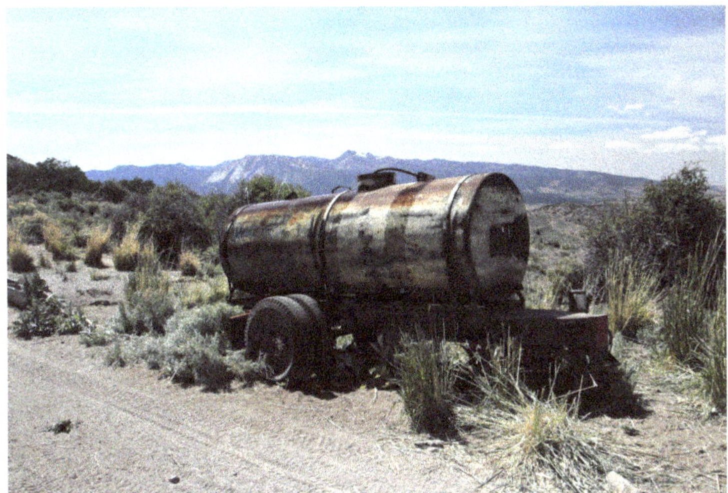

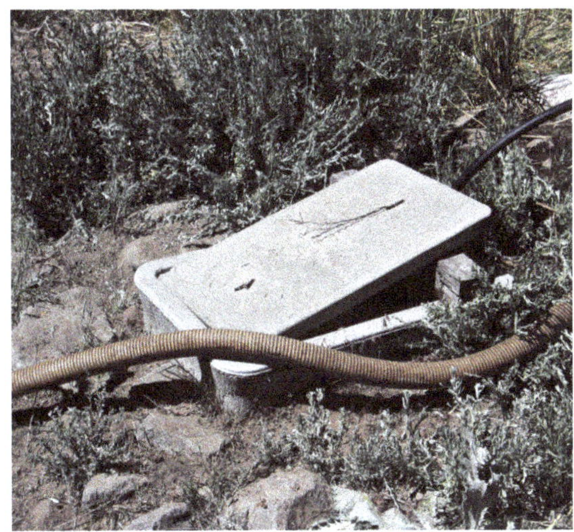

Guzzler near Five Mile Reservoir set
up to water wildlife in the area

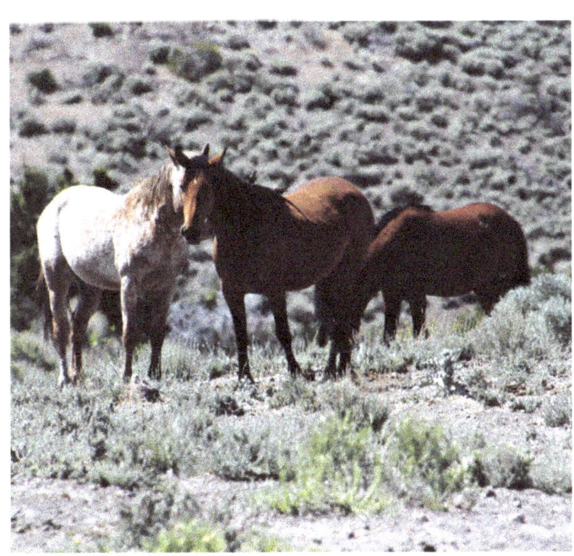

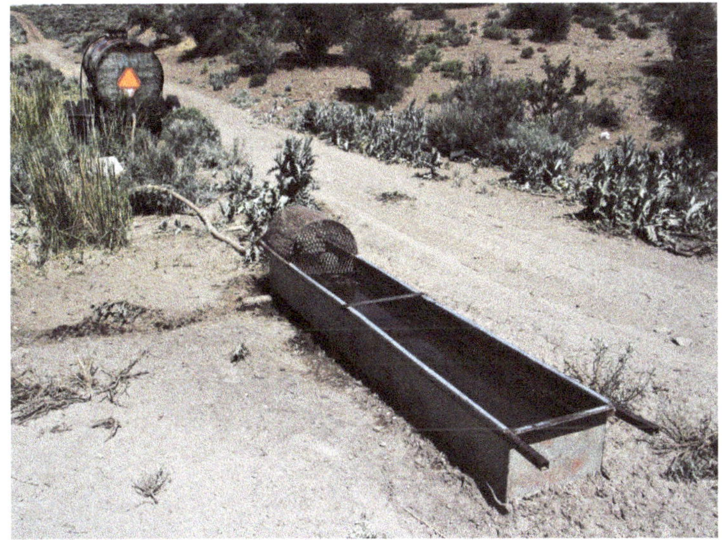

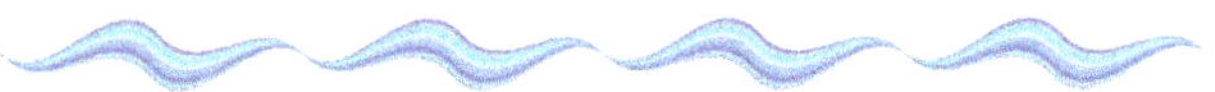

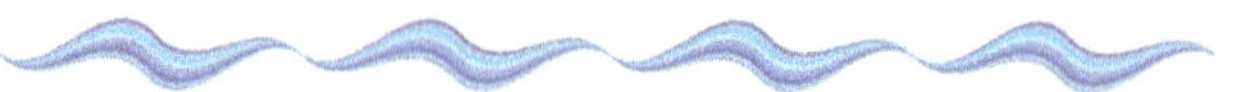

Five Mile Reservoir and
Ice House c. 1877

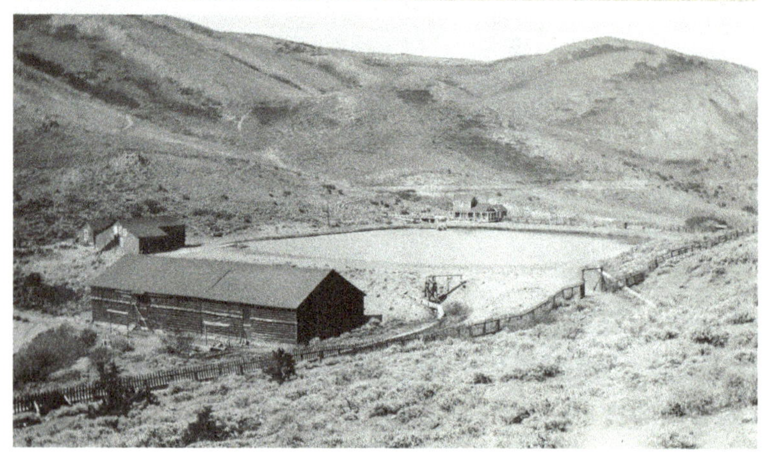

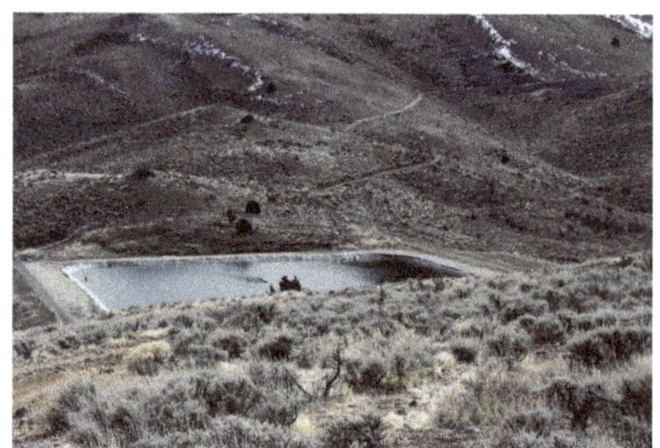

Five Mile Reservoir

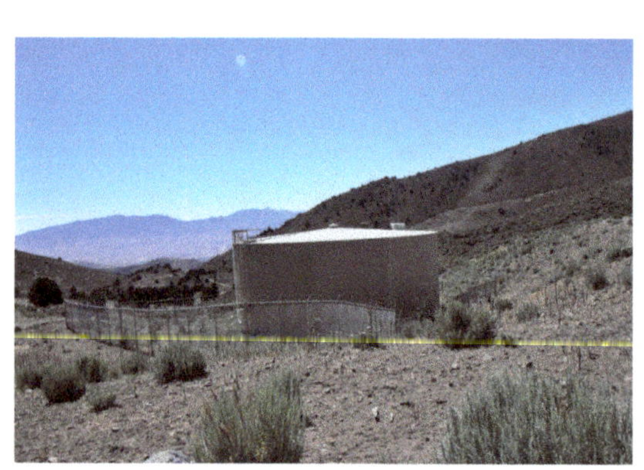

Five Mile Reservoir Tank

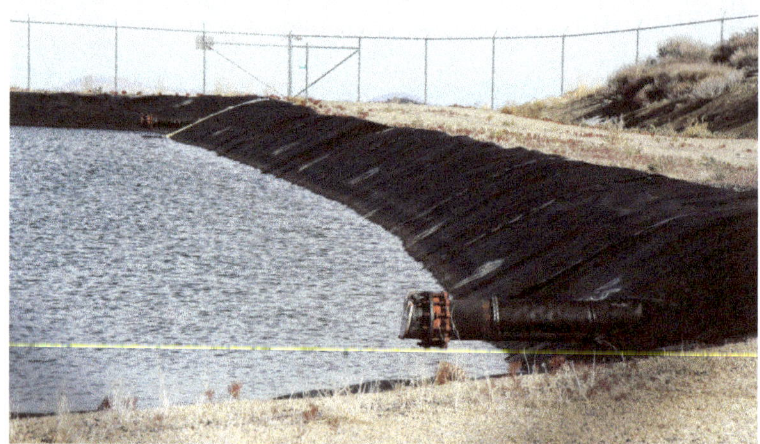

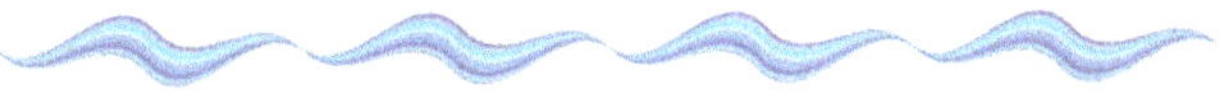

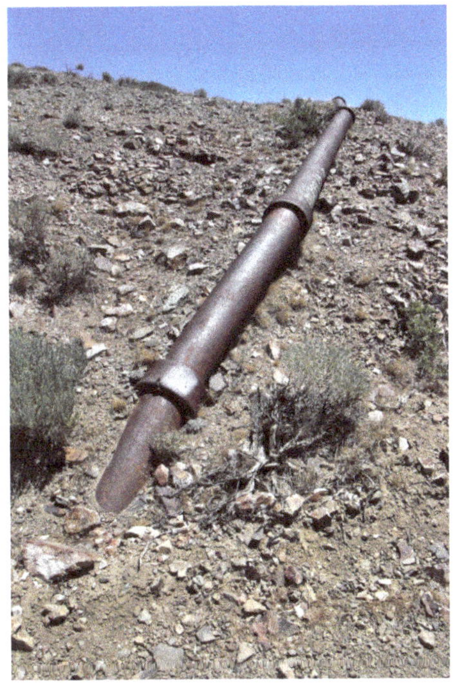

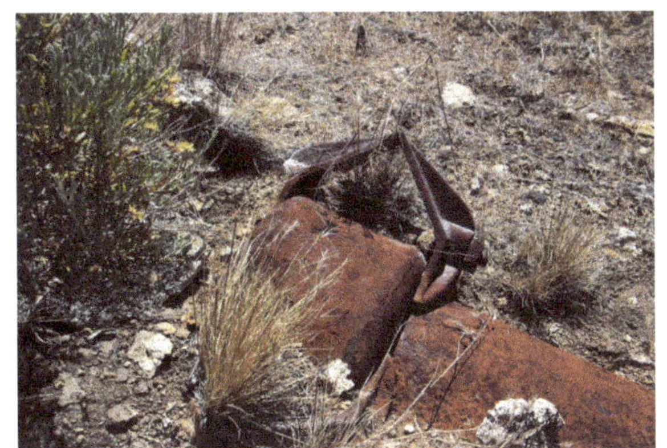

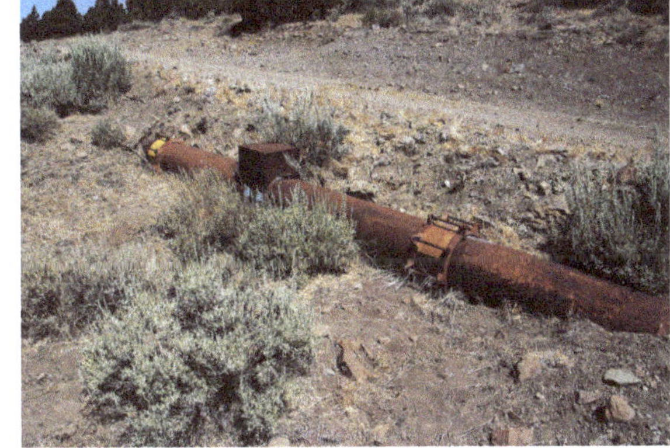

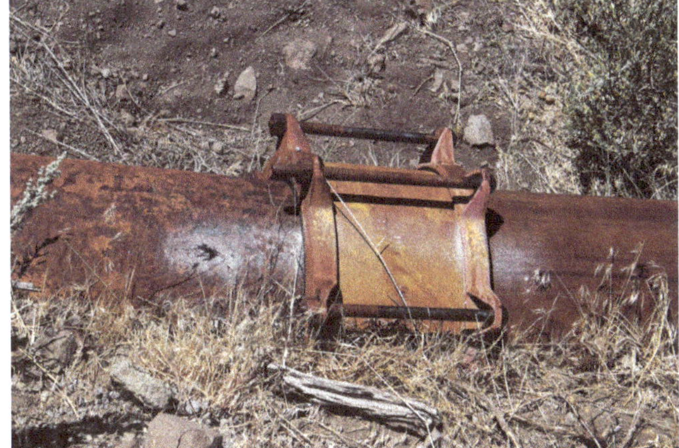

Different types of repair
couplers from Five Mile
Reservoir to Virginia City

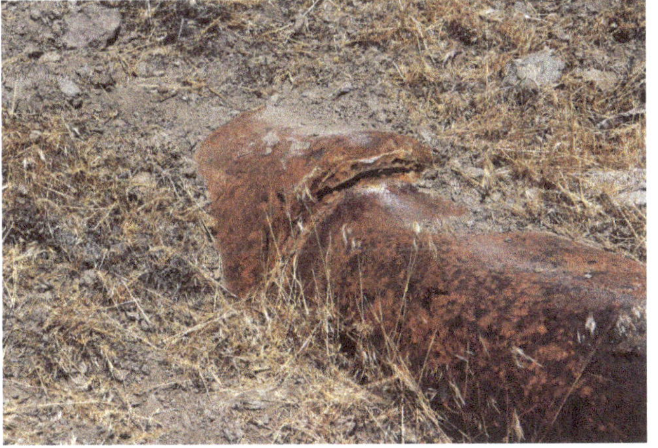

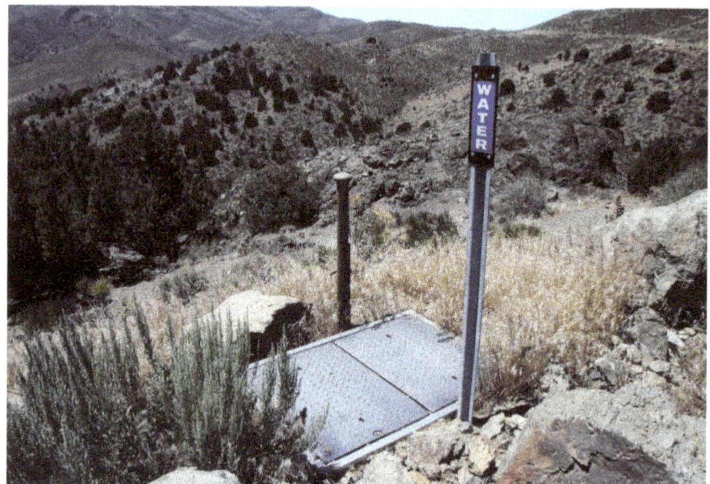

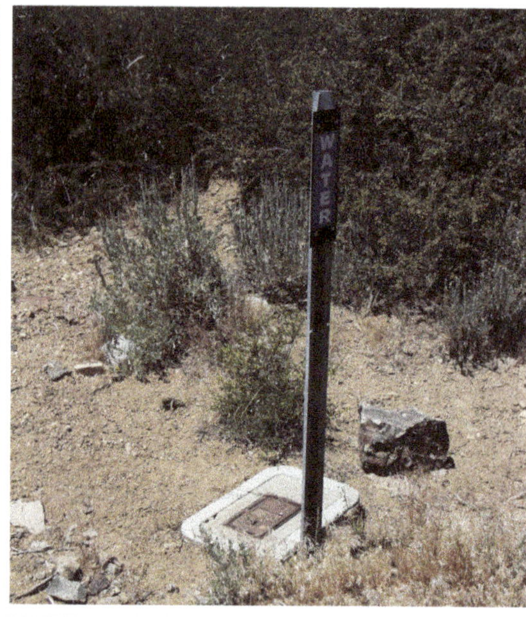

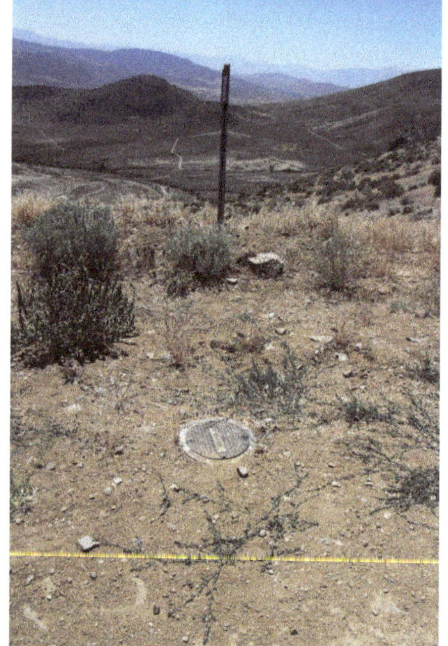

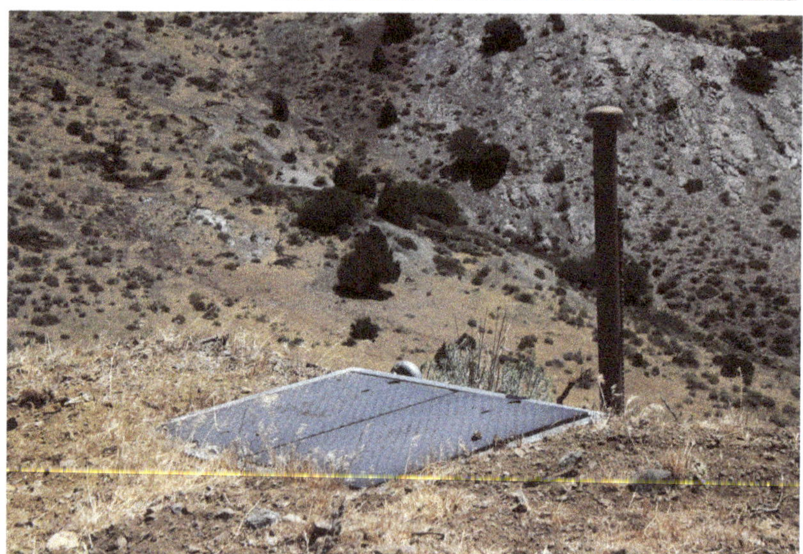

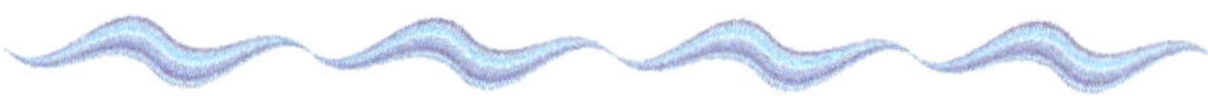

Different types of water boxes from Five Mile Reservoir to Virginia City

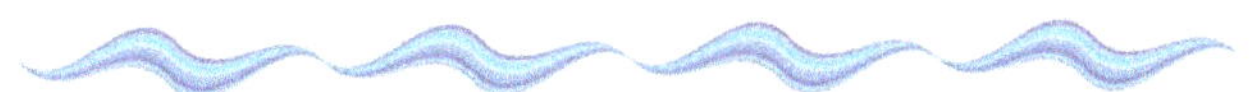

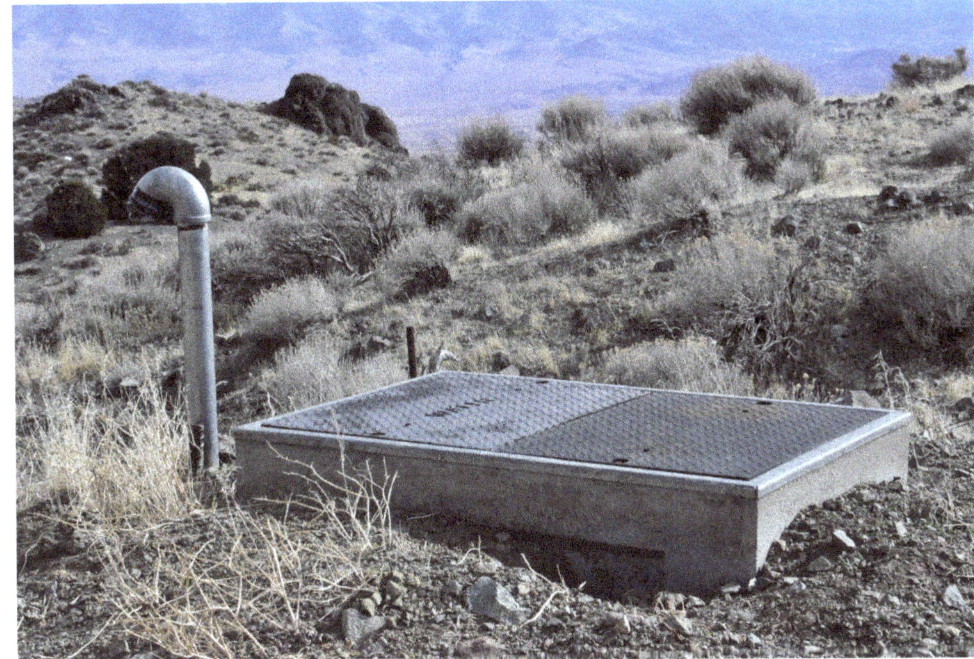

Air Release Valve

Guzzler near Five
Mile Reservoir

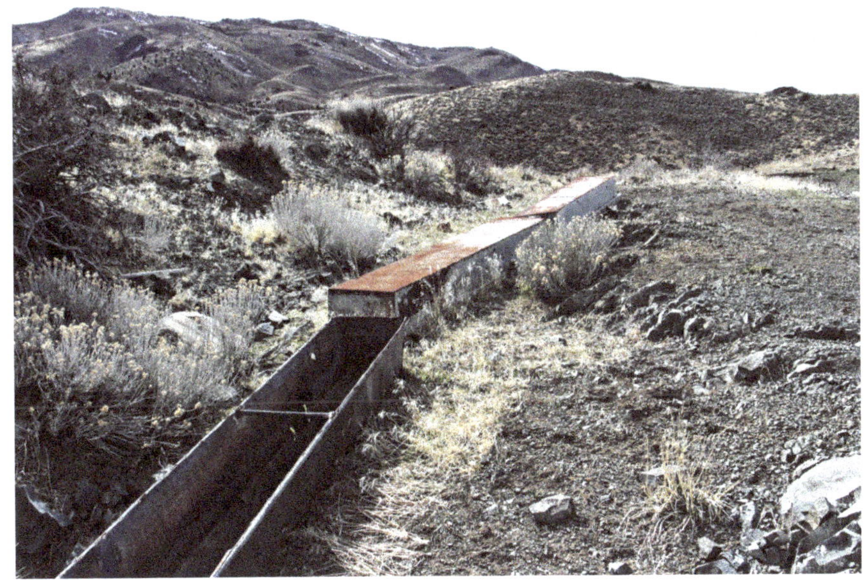

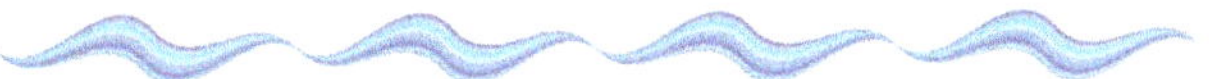

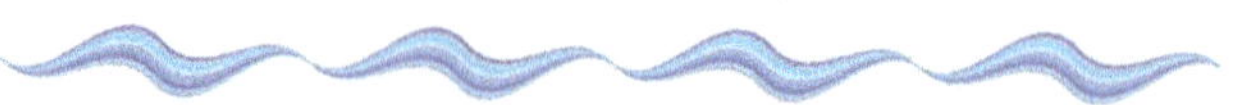

Virginia City
Water Tanks

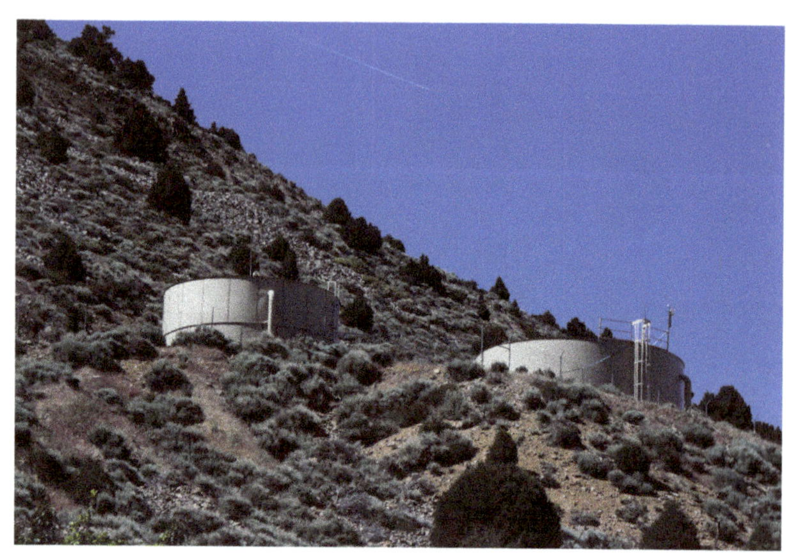

Bullion Tank is located on top
of the old Bullion Mine

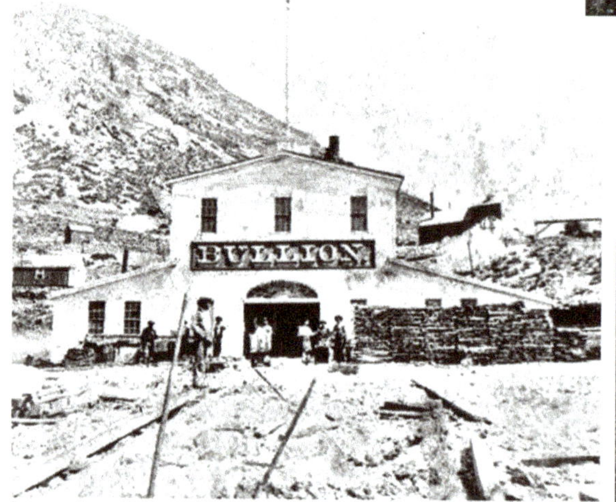

Bullion Mine in 1866

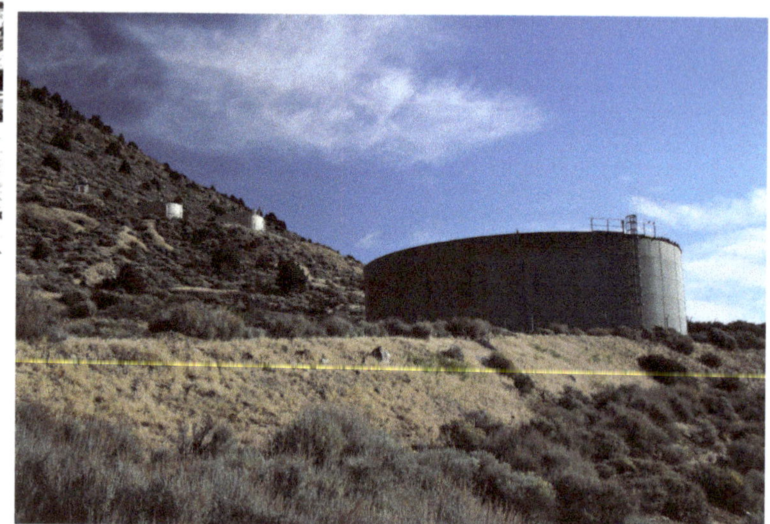

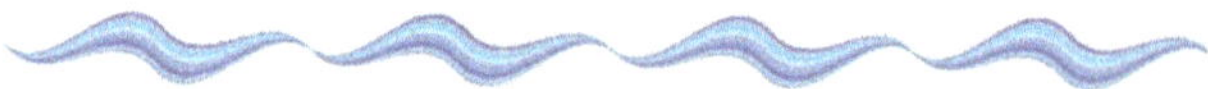

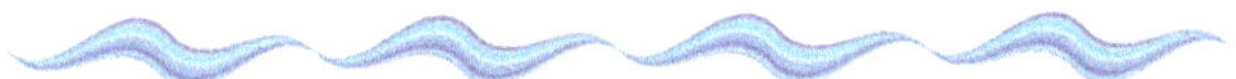

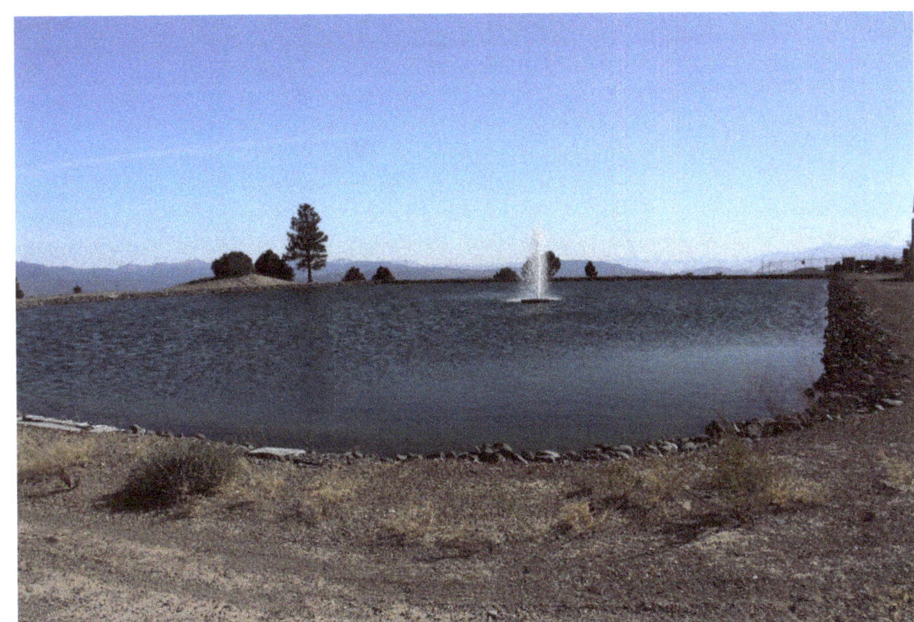

End of the line.
Divide Reservoir in
Virginia City

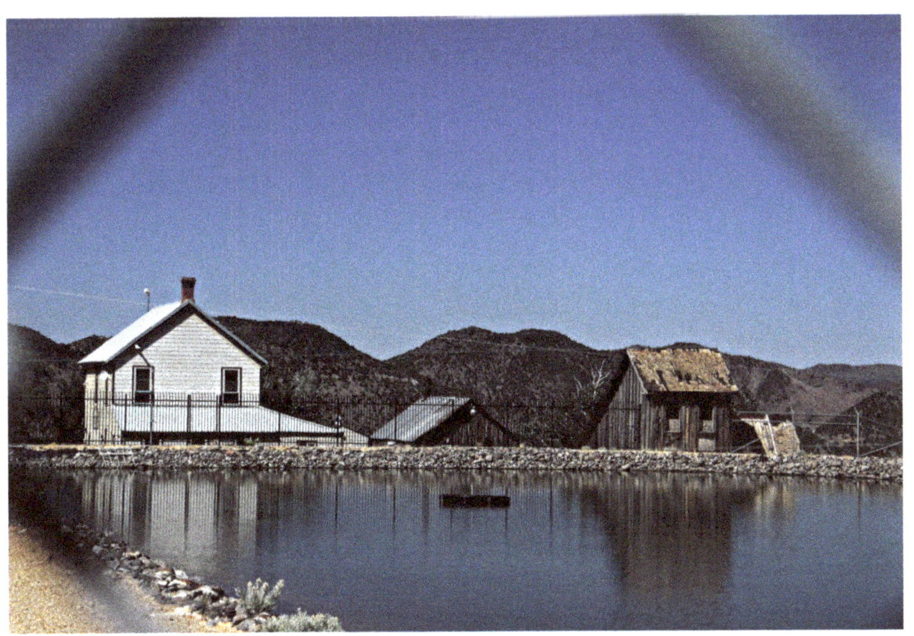

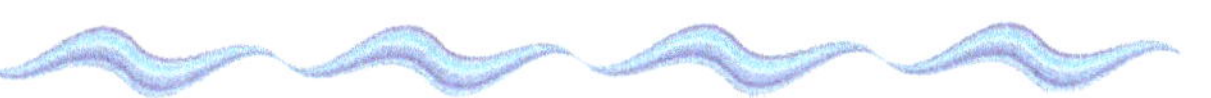

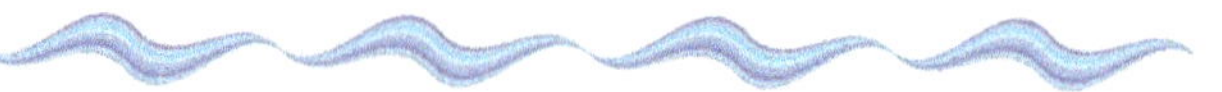

Offshoot of the water system near Gold Hill Nevada

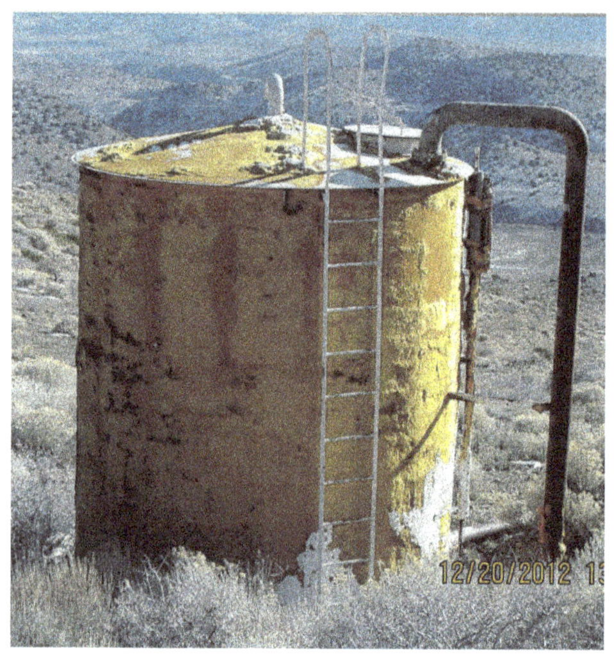

Upper water tank

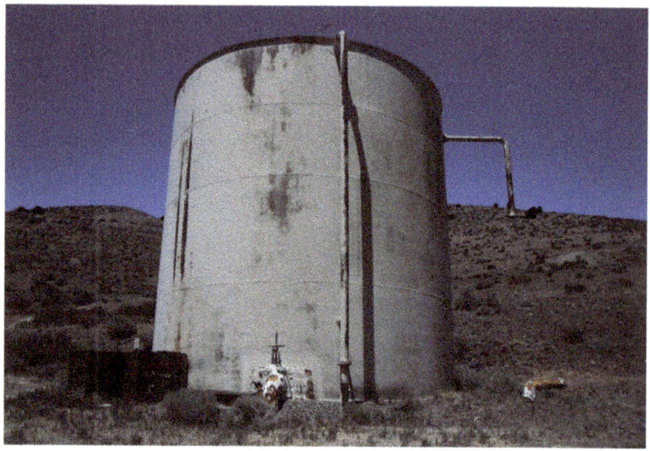

Lower water tank

Upper water tank provided water to the lower water tank for Comstock Mining Inc.

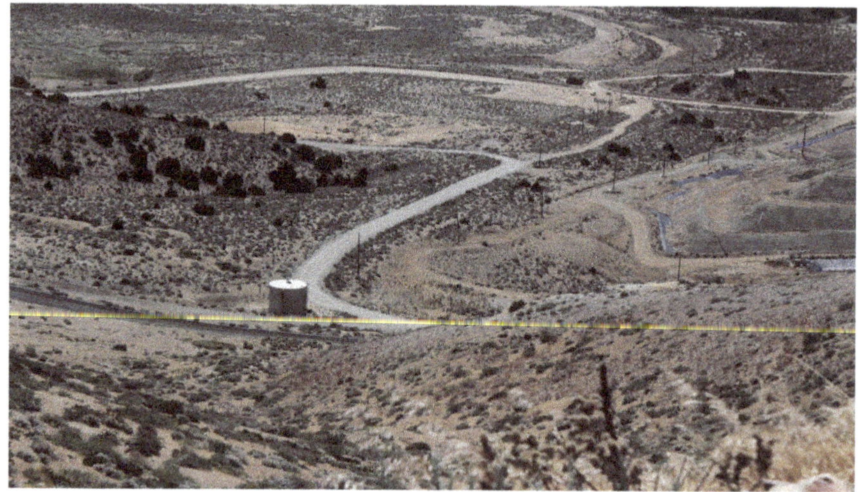

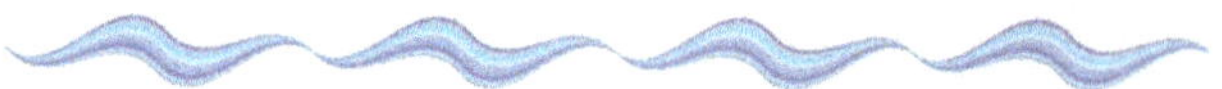

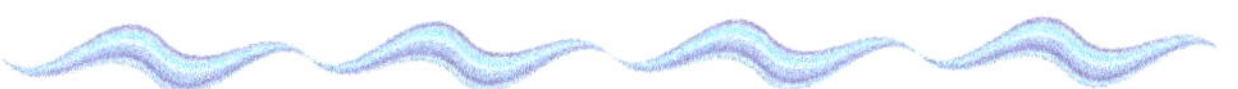

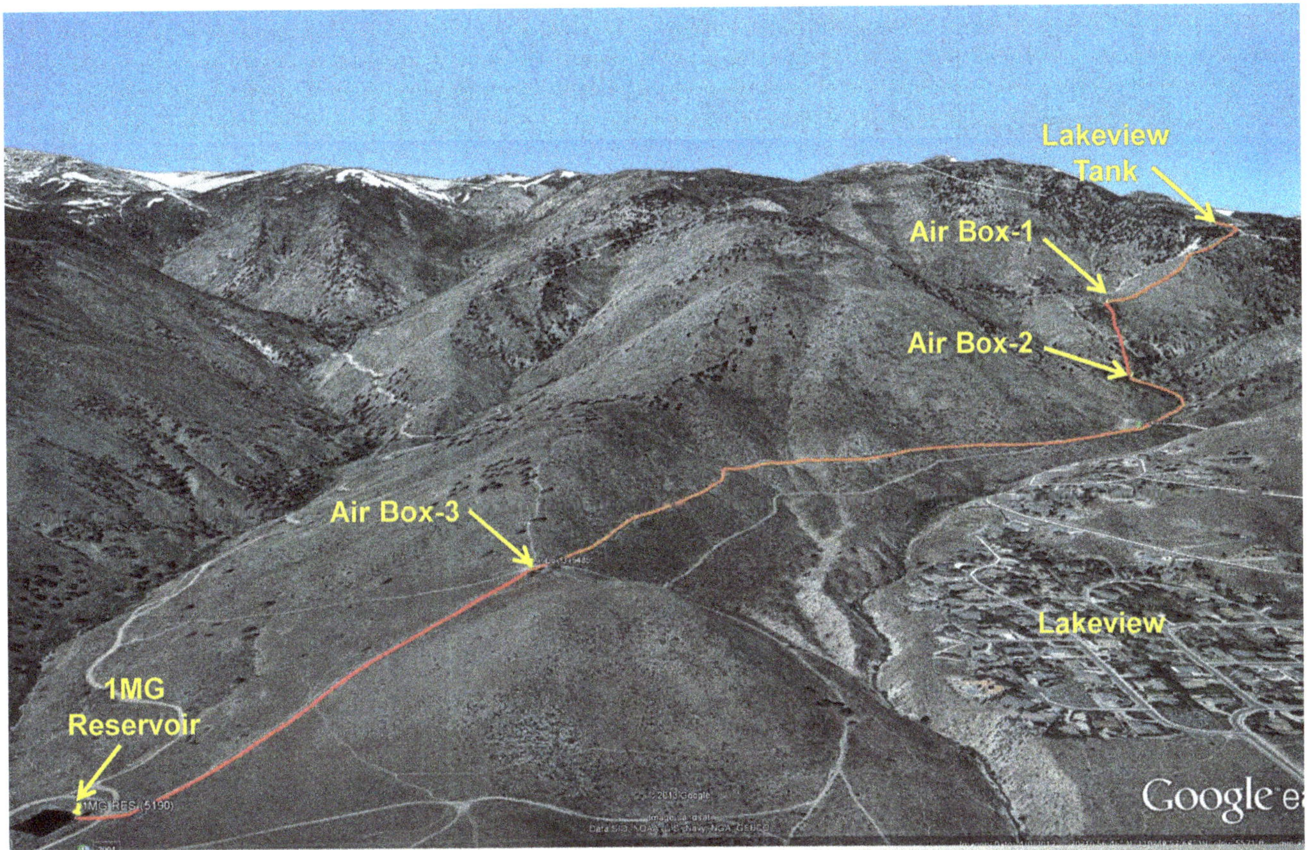

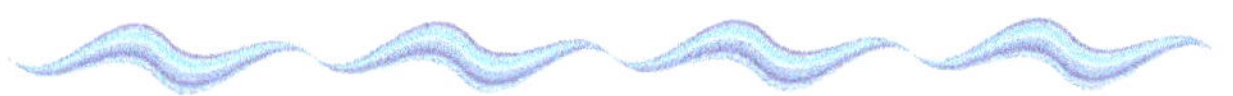

Air Boxes (Lakeview Tank to 1MG Lined Reservoir)

Carson City line from Lakeview Tank

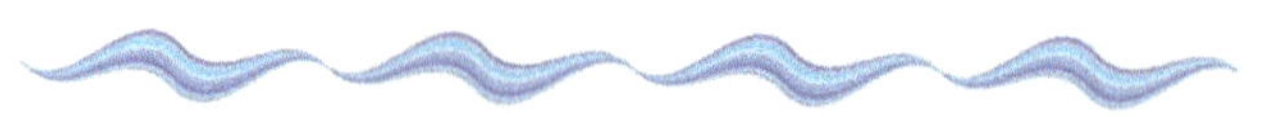

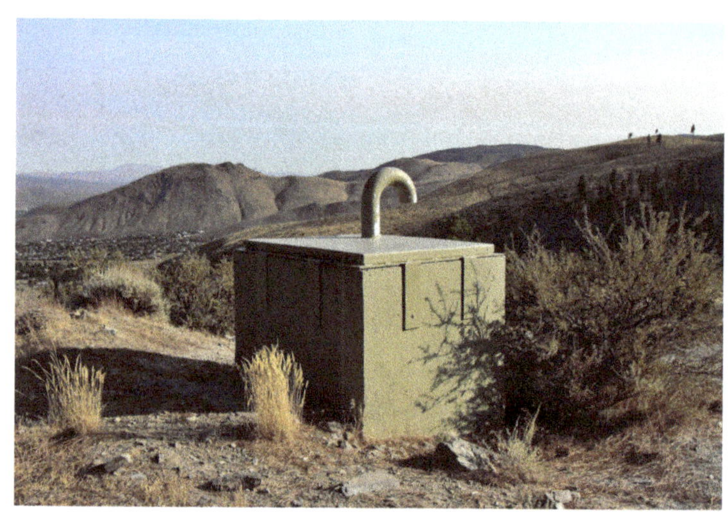

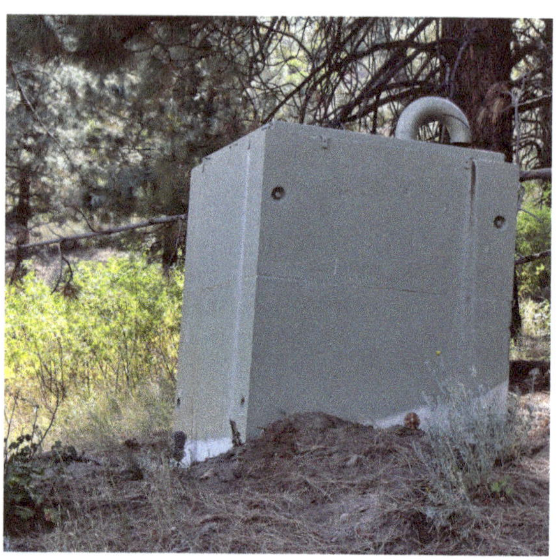

Air Boxes on the Carson line Numbers 1, 2 and 3

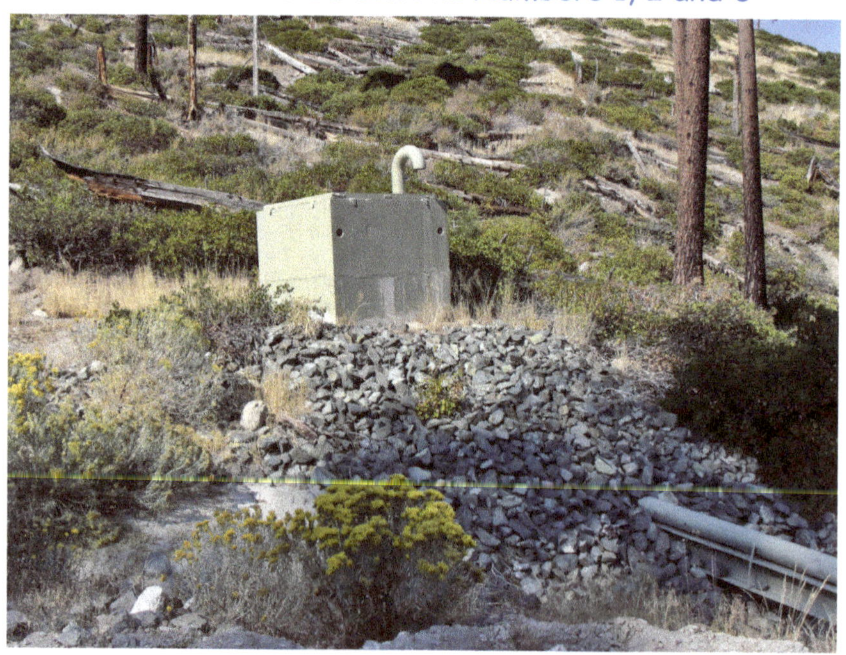

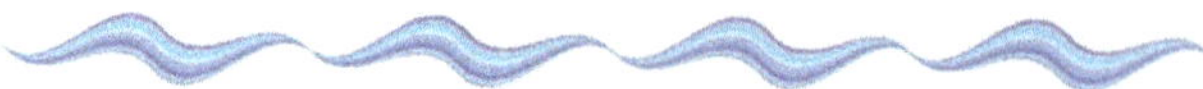

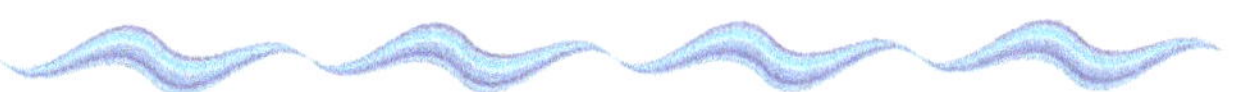

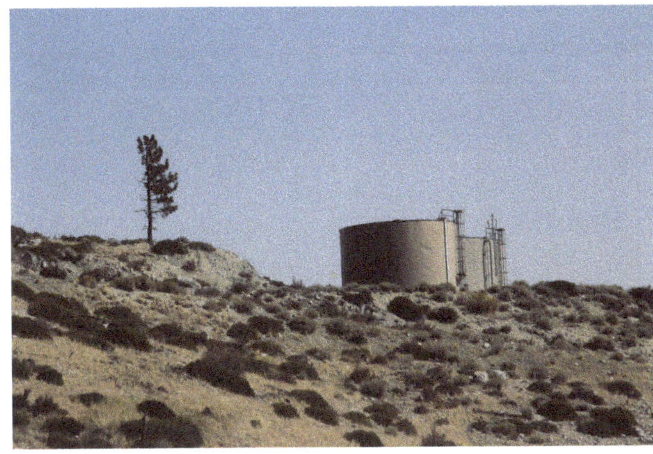

Timberline water
tanks holding water
for Carson City

Carson City
One Million Gallon
Reservoir

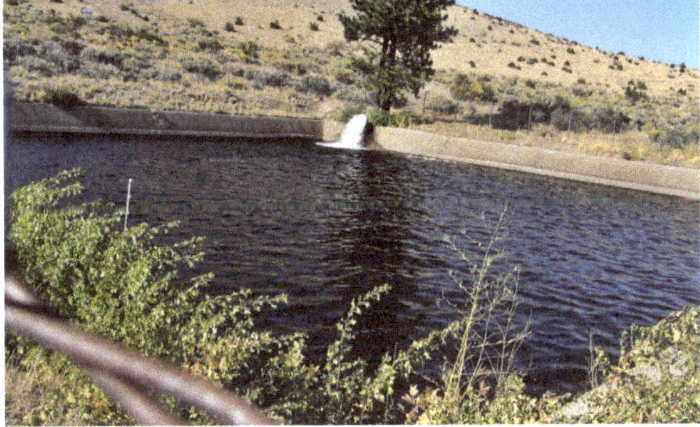

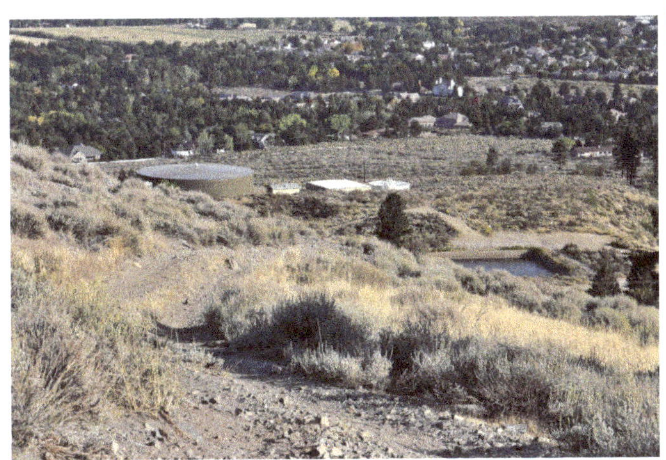

Carson City Water Tanks

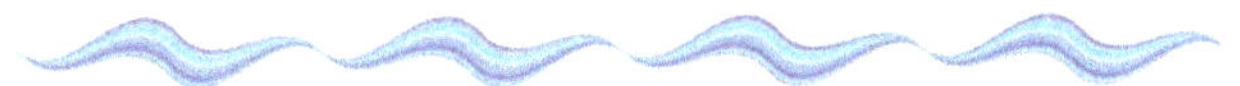

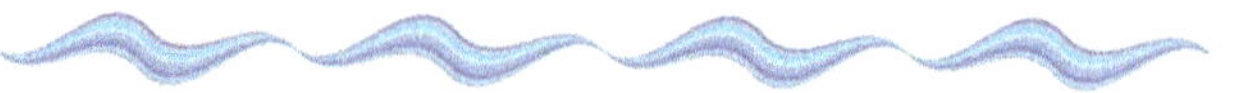

The drive up Ash Canyon

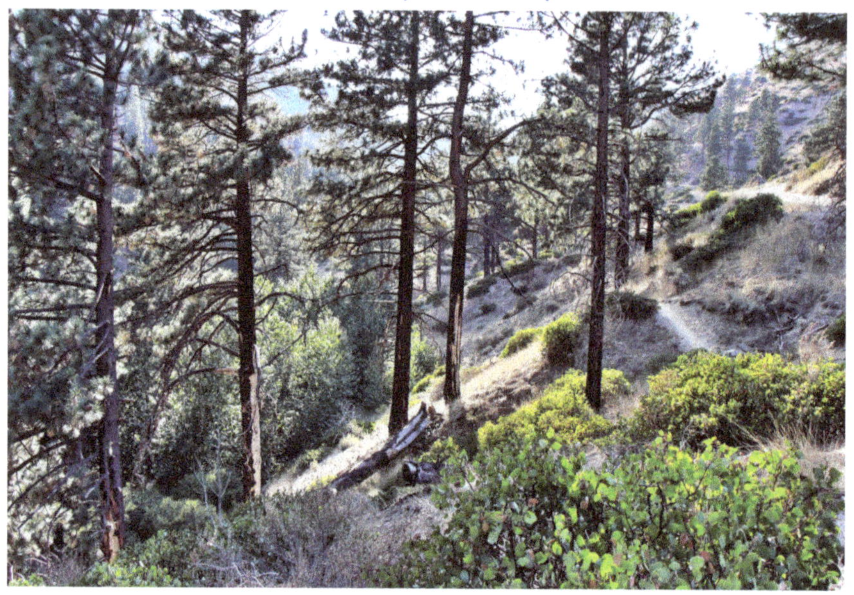

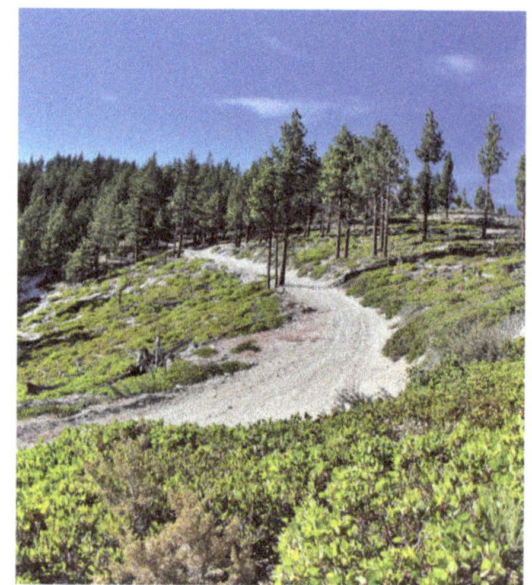

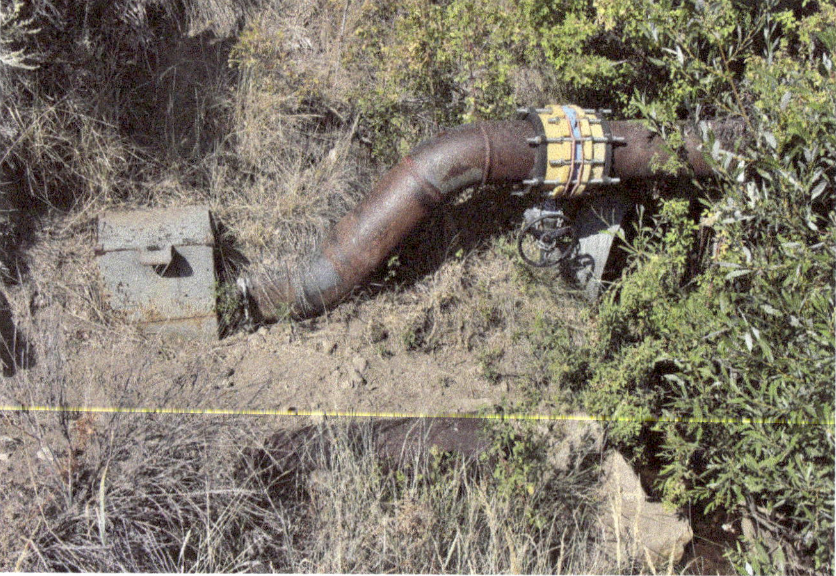

A section of the old pipe
on the Carson City line

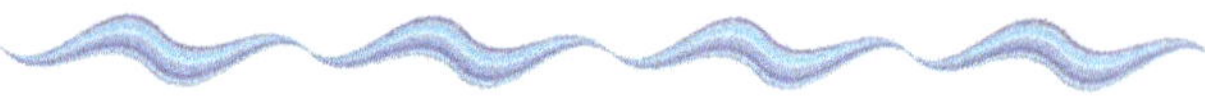

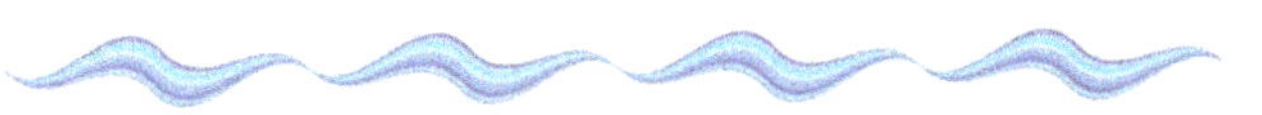

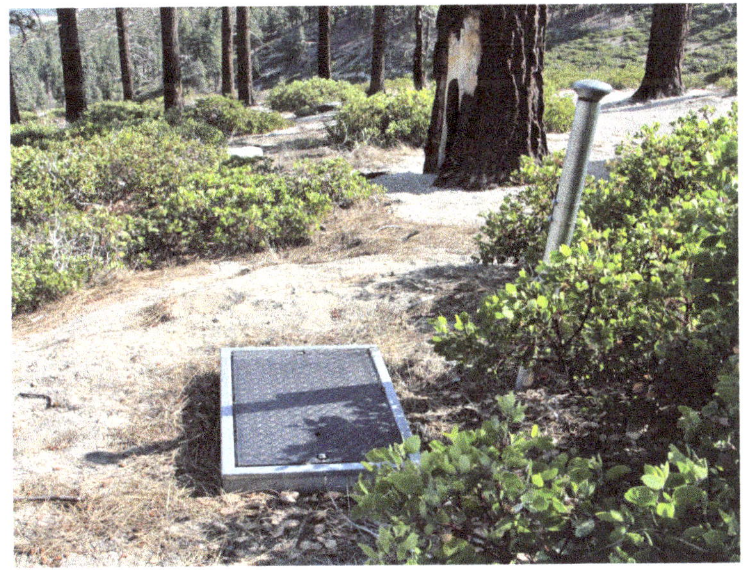

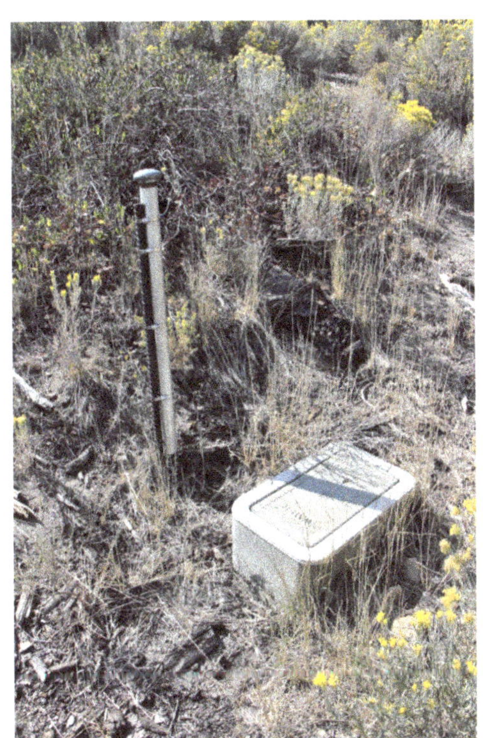

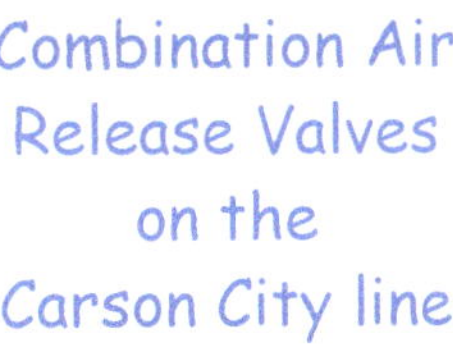

Combination Air
Release Valves
on the
Carson City line

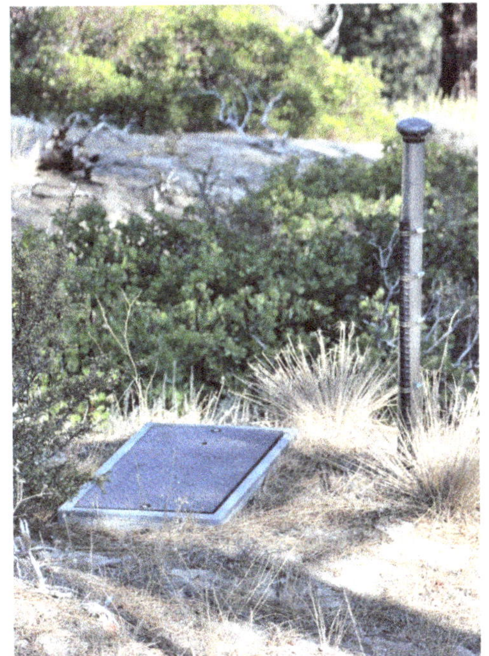

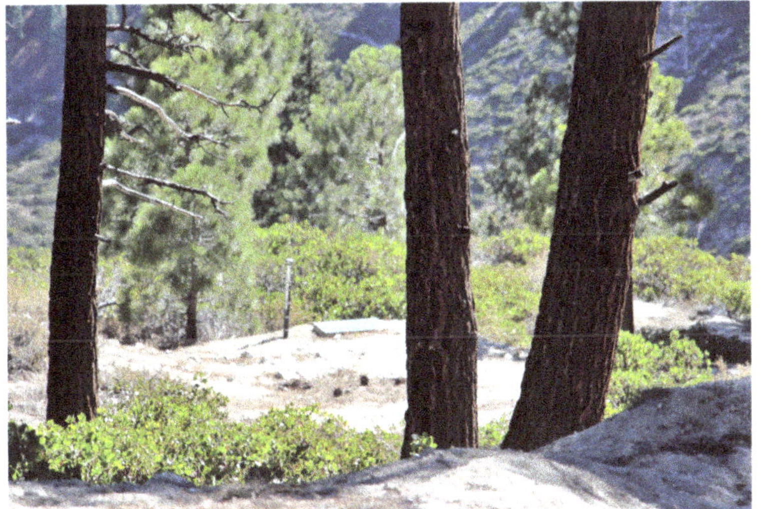

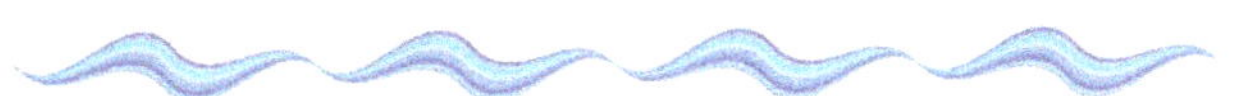

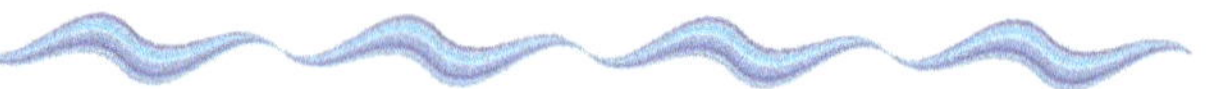

Near the top of Ash Canyon with a view of
Hobart Creek Reservoir

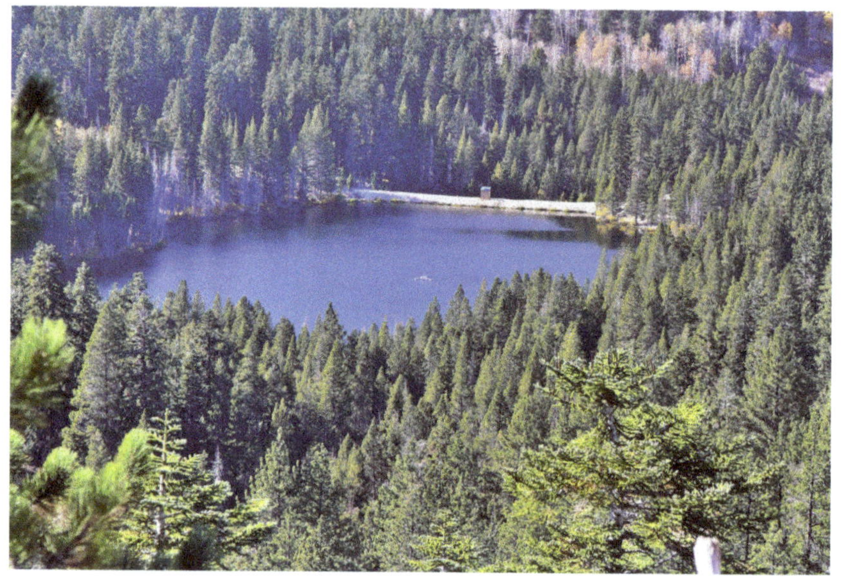

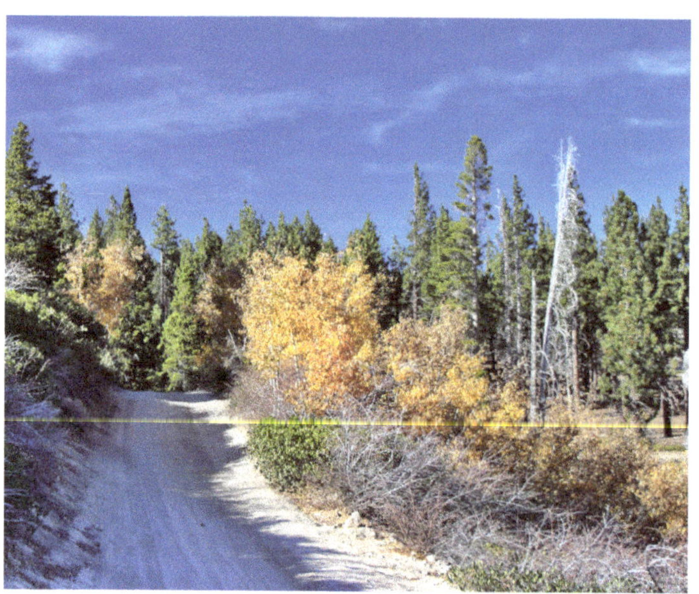

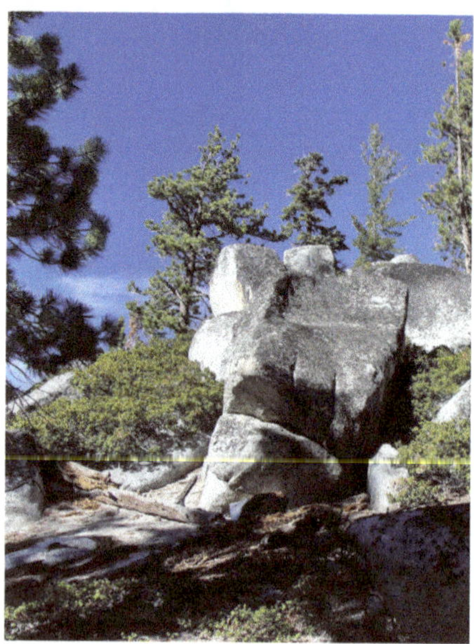

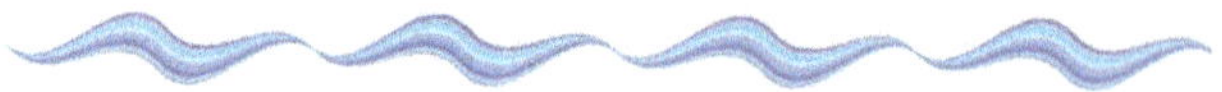

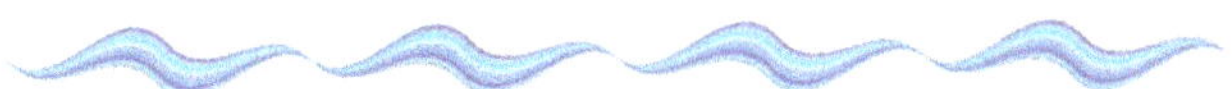

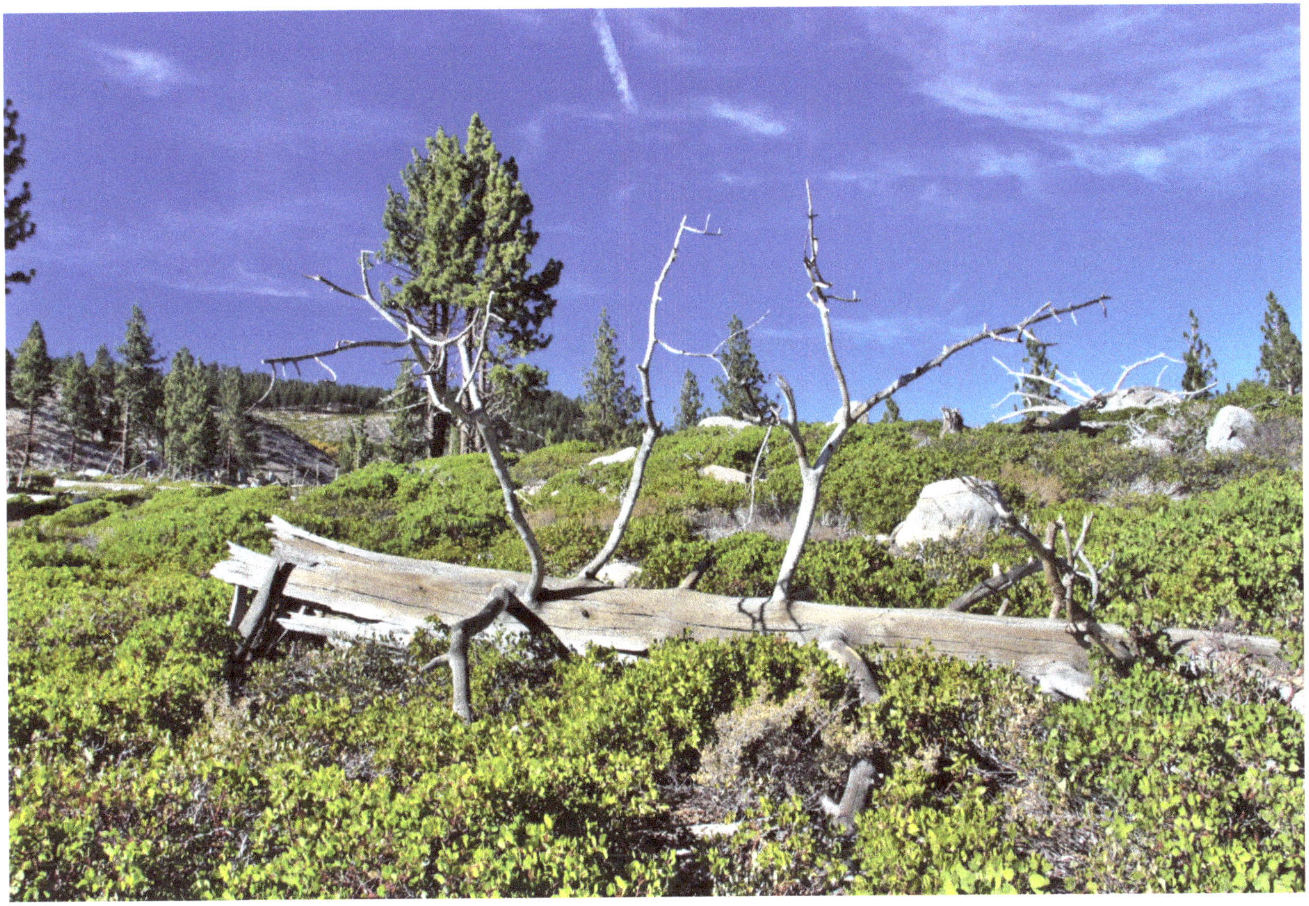

Beautiful Memories
Marlette Water System

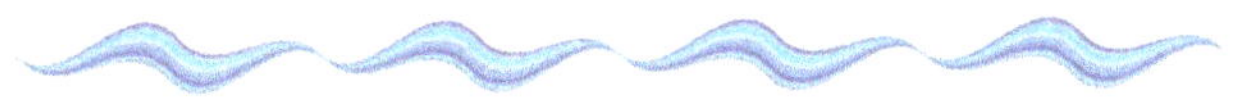

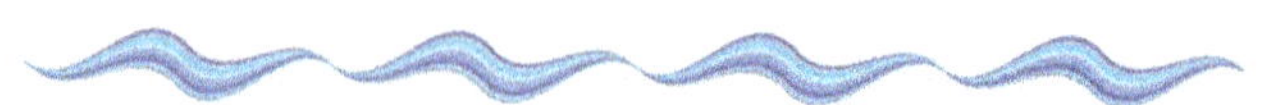

References

History of Nevada 1881
Thompson and West

History of Nevada
Edited by Sam P. Davis
Volume I and II

The Journals of Alfred Doten 1849 – 1903
Edited by Walter Van Tilburg Clark

Water Supply for the Comstock
Hugh A. Shamberger, 1969

The Marlette Lake Water System
Legislative Commission of the Legislative
Counsel
February 1969
Bulletin No. 69

History of Nevada
2nd Edition Revised
Russell R. Elliott
1973 and 1987 University of Nebraska
Press

Saga of Lake Tahoe
E. B. Scott
Book 1 and 2
Under Marlette Lake

Historic Marlette Water System
NV Rural Water Association
May 24, 2016
Tahoe Oversite Committee
December 18, 2017

Oral History from Pete Lenord

Carson City Apple Tree Newspaper
August 31, 1980

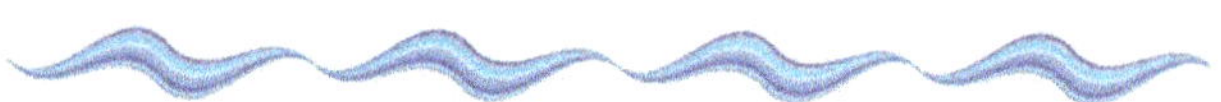

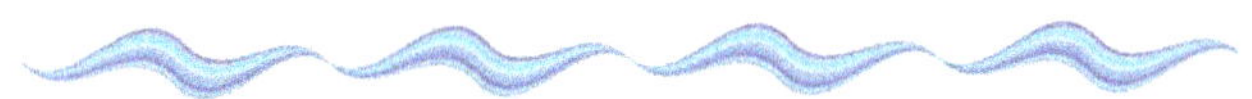

About the Author

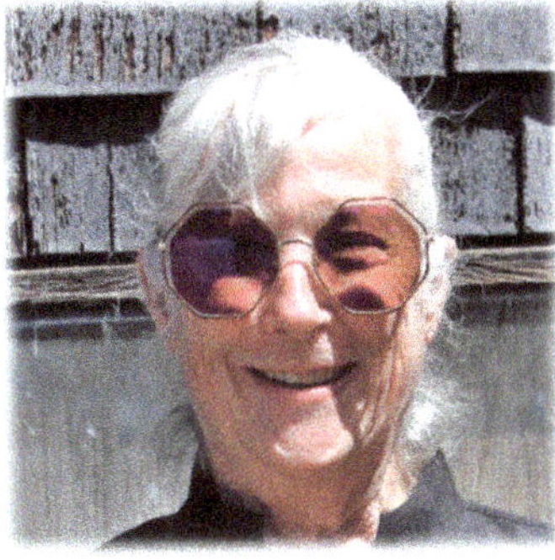

Julie Michler is a freelance photographer and historian specializing in old ghost towns, pioneer cemeteries and historical areas. She started in photography as a teenager taking landscape pictures with her point and shoot camera.

In 1972 Julie received her first Single Lens Reflex camera. From there she branched out into taking pictures of ghost towns and pioneer cemeteries in California and Nevada.   In the early 2000's she became interested in Native American Rock Art. That lead her into a whole new venture in photography. She has produced many small books of her travel adventures for family and friends.

In 2017 Julie moved to Reno where she started working with people who were restoring the Sutro Tunnel in Dayton, Nevada, where she really started getting involved in the history of Nevada. Then Julie moved to Carson City. She started visiting the Marlette Lake area which is only accessible by hiking or horseback riding. She started out taking pictures of this pristine area just for herself. This morphed into something bigger and she became interested in the history of the water system.

Julie started to incorporate this history into a picture book just for herself. She has traveled all the roads in the water system from Marlette to Virginia City, Nevada and it has been quite a trip. She has been able to go into the back country that most people don't get to see. Julie is very excited to be able to share her experiences with other people as the Marlette area provides its beauty and tranquility for the world to enjoy

Julie has studied Photography, Native American Rock Art, Mining History of the Comstock. and Nevada Ghost Towns. Carson City, Nevada is her home. She shares her home with her partner Dan and with her three desert dogs, Malibu, Miss Mazie, TareeToo and two cats. In her spare time she deals poker at a casino in Reno, Nevada.

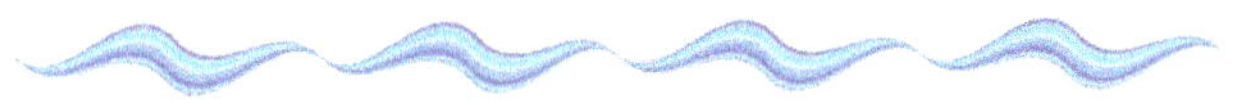